剑桥KET考试
阅读通关周计划

金利／编著

化学工业出版社
·北京·

图书在版编目（CIP）数据

剑桥KET考试阅读通关周计划 / 金利编著. —北京：
化学工业出版社，2024.6
（剑桥KET考试通关周计划）
ISBN 978-7-122-45346-4

Ⅰ.①剑… Ⅱ.①金… Ⅲ.①英语水平考试–阅读教
学–自学参考资料 Ⅳ.①H310.41

中国国家版本馆CIP数据核字（2024）第067666号

责任编辑：马小桐 马 骄　　　　　　装帧设计：张 辉
责任校对：杜杏然　　　　　　　　　　版式设计：梧桐影

出版发行：化学工业出版社
　　　　　（北京市东城区青年湖南街13号 邮政编码100011）
印　　装：河北京平诚乾印刷有限公司
787mm×1092mm 1/16 印张10 字数177千字
2024年6月北京第1版第1次印刷

购书咨询：010-64518888　　　　　售后服务：010-64518899
网　　址：http://www.cip.com.cn
凡购买本书，如有缺损质量问题，本社销售中心负责调换。

定　　价：49.90元　　　　　　　　　　版权所有　违者必究

前言

　　《剑桥KET考试阅读通关周计划》一书写给正在备考剑桥A2 Key(KET)阅读考试的考生。我们深知准备阅读考试需要一定的时间规划、答题技巧、考点锦囊以及充分练习。因此，本书采用讲解与规划相结合的学习方法，将这些要素有机地结合在一起，帮助考生顺利通关。

　　⏱ KET考试阅读通关 = **合理的时间规划 + 思路点拨 + 考点锦囊 + 每周一练**

★ 8周学习规划

　　按周规划好学习内容，跟着规划学，易坚持，更高效。

　　本书学习内容以周为单位，从考试内容入手，为考生规划好要学习或练习的内容，跟着规划走，利用碎片化时间来学习，用时少，效率高。

　　◇【周目标】每周开启学习前，了解本周学习目标。

　　◇【周中学】每周周中学习考试核心备考知识，掌握答题思路，积累考试词句。

　　◇【周末练】周六周日，集中演练本周所学。

　　一周内容，以目标为导向，学练结合，知识掌握更加扎实。

★ 思路点拨 + 考点锦囊

　　考题呈现，剖析答题思路，分享KET阅读锦囊，答题更容易。

　　在每周学习中，针对考试中的考题题型，本书都给出了答题的思路以及窍门（如先读题、划出关键词等）；此外，本书还会针对每种题型，给出相关的同义转述词汇、固定搭配或语法考点。

本书旨在帮助考生建立答题思维，而非死记硬背，有思路，有方法，有技巧积累，考场答题更从容。

★ **每周一练 + 全真模拟**

多样化题型操练本周所学，学后巩固练习，知识掌握更加扎实。

本书的练习题包括各种多样化的阅读题型，如单项选择、选词填空、句子翻译等，多维度操练本周所学内容，进一步夯实所学，打好基础，帮助考生有效备考。

通过每周一练和全真模拟题，考生将能够熟悉各种考试题型，锻炼阅读基础能力，并在实践中提高应对考试的信心。

总之，本书致力于为考生提供全面而高效的学习资源，让考生在备考剑桥A2 Key(KET)阅读考试时更有信心、更具竞争力。希望通过本书的学习，考生能够顺利通过考试，实现自己的考试目标。

目录

熟悉考试

第1周目标

学习模块	时间	主题	内容	
	Day 1	考试概述	考试要求及评分标准	☐
	Day 2	备考贴士	熟悉答题卡、备考建议等	☐
	Day 3	短信息选择题	题型详解、答题技巧、样题举例	☐
熟悉考试	Day 4	信息匹配题	题型详解、答题技巧、样题举例	☐
	Day 5	阅读理解题	题型详解、答题技巧、样题举例	☐
	Day 6	完形填空题	题型详解、答题技巧、样题举例	☐
	Day 7	语法填空题	题型详解、答题技巧、样题举例	☐

Day 1 考试概述

考试介绍

剑桥通用英语五级证书考试，即Main Suite Examinations (MSE)，为英国剑桥大学考试委员会设计的英语作为外国语的五级系列考试。

A2 Key for Schools为五级考试中的第一级，即更名前的"KET青少版"考试。该考试对应CEFR的A2级别。通过A2 Key for Schools考试的考生能够达到以下水平。

➢ 能够理解并运用基础词组和表达。

➢ 能够理解简单的英语文本。

➢ 能够用英语进行自我介绍并回答有关个人详细信息的基本问题。

➢ 在熟悉的情景中，使用英语进行沟通。

➢ 理解简短的通知和简单的口头指示，可以书写简短的便条。

其中，"阅读和写作"部分是A2 Key for Schools的第一套试卷。

✓ 阅读考题分为5个部分，共计30小题。

✓ 阅读和写作整体考试时长为60分钟，其中阅读答题时间建议40分钟，包括填涂答题卡时间。

✓ 阅读部分卷面分数为30分，会被换算成剑桥英语分数量表分数，即标准分。

🎧 题型及分值

阅读部分分为5个部分，主要任务包括：

➢ 阅读短信息，选择符合信息内容的选项；

➢ 阅读短文，进行信息匹配、完成多道选择题；

➢ 阅读长文章，完成多道选择题；

➢ 阅读一篇事实类短文，进行完形填空；

➢ 阅读邮件，填空。

阅读5种题型及具体分值比例如下。

Part 部分	Task Types 题型	Sample 样例截图	Number of Questions 题目数量	Number of Marks 分数
Part 1	3-option multiple choice 阅读6条短信息，选择符合信息内容的选项		6	6

续表

Part 部分	Task Types 题型	Sample 样例截图	Number of Questions 题目数量	Number of Marks 分数
Part 2	3-option multiple matching 阅读同一主题的3篇短文和7个问题，进行信息匹配		7	7
Part 3	3-option multiple choice 阅读1篇长文章，完成5道选择题		5	5
Part 4	3-option multiple choice cloze 阅读一篇事实类的短文，选择恰当选项，完形填空		6	6
Part 5	Open cloze 补全邮件(有时包括回复邮件)，每小题填一个单词		6	6
总计			30	30

🎧 **评分标准**

　　阅读部分共计30题，每题1分，满分30分。根据剑桥考试计分规则，A2 Key for Schools 考试四部分（阅读、写作、听力、口语）各个部分的计分成绩总分是150分，综合成绩是将所有单项分数加总除以四计算得出。其中阅读部分的30分折合成150分的计分分值如下。

阅读部分卷面分数	剑桥考试标准分数	CEFR级别
30	150	Level B1+
28	140	Level B1
20	120	Level A2
13	100	Level A1
7	82*	—

＊ A2 Key for Schools考试报告的最低分数

Day 2　备考贴士

🎧 熟悉答题卡

阅读考试填涂答题卡需使用B或HB铅笔。

1. 考生的基本个人信息在答题卡中已打印好，考生需要核对个人信息，如果信息正确无误，将自己姓名全拼抄写到【Candidate Signature】框内即可（姓名的拼音需全部大写）。

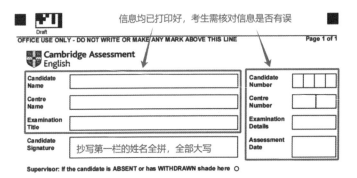

2. 答题卡具体填涂说明。

> 选择题（Part 1、Part 2、Part 3、Part 4），将对应选项圆圈涂满、涂黑。

> Part 5书写答案时，全部字母都需要大写。

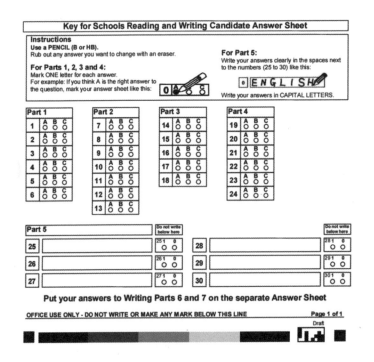

备考建议

在准备阅读部分时，需要注意以下几点。

考试进行中

- ➢ 仔细阅读文章并审题，确保你回答了所有问题，不要看到一个词就选择答案。
- ➢ 如果有不认识的单词也无须太过担心，试着猜猜它们的意思。
- ➢ 即使你对某些答案不是很确定，也要答完所有题目。为每一道题选一个答案。
- ➢ 慢慢来，不要着急，你有足够的时间回答所有的问题。
- ➢ 检查答案并且确保它们都写在了答题卡的正确位置。
- ➢ 如果你发现填写错误，请用橡皮擦掉。

平时积累

- ➢ 多样化阅读材料：可以选择一些难度适宜的通知、电子邮件、短信、文章等，进行阅读训练，比如朗读、跟读、背诵、挖空练习等。
- ➢ 词汇积累：按照主题分类记忆单词，如假期、旅行、运动、活动、人物经历等，都是阅读中经常考到的主题。
- ➢ 语法知识积累：了解英语的基本语法规则，如名词、代词、介词、冠词等，熟悉常见用法和固定搭配。

Day 3 　短信息选择题

题型分析

【题型】短信息选择题，单选，三选一

【题量】6题

【内容】6条短信息，包括短邮件、标识、通知、短信和广告等不同类型的内容。每道题有一则短信息和三个文本选项

【要求】阅读6条短信息，选择符合信息内容的选项

【样例】

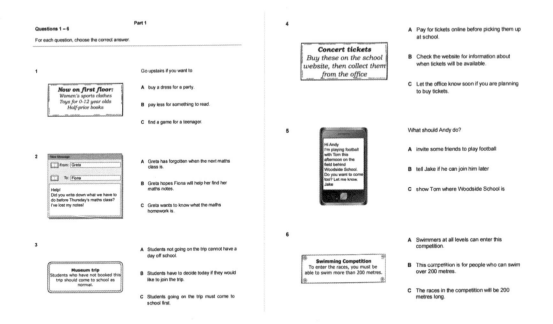

答题技巧

核心考点

✓ 题目主要考查考生对日常生活中出现的一些短信息的理解能力，包括邮件、标识、通知、短信、广告等。

答题步骤与建议

1. 阅读短信息，根据视觉信息（布局、位置等）确认其出现的语境，并划出关键词，比如时间、地点、人物等。

2. 阅读短信息右边的三个选项，然后划出关键信息。

3. 回到短信息，匹配合适的选项。

4. 如果遇到内容相近的迷惑选项，应将两者纵向对比，辨别两者之间的不同，从而选出正确选项。

样题解析

For each question, choose the correct answer.

Concert tickets

Buy these on the school website, then collect them from the office

A Pay for tickets online before picking them up at school.

B Check the website for information about when tickets will be available.

C Let the office know soon if you are planning to buy tickets.

解析

Step 1:【审图片，划重点】

Concert tickets

Buy these on the school website, then collect them from the office

- 关键信息：Concert tickets（音乐会门票）。
- 文本分析：音乐会门票通知。
- 核心句拆解：Buy these on the school website，其中these指代concert tickets，即"在学校网站上购买音乐会门票"。collect them from the office，collect常用意思为"收集"，此处意为"领取"，句意为"到办公室领取（音乐会门票）"。

Step 2:【审选项，找匹配】

1. 关键信息

   A：Pay for tickets online before picking them up at school.

   B：Check the website for information about when tickets will be available.

   C：Let the office know soon if you are planning to buy tickets.

2. 选项解析

   A：在去学校取票之前先在网上付款。

   B：在网站上查询什么时候可以买到票。

   C：如果你打算买票，请尽快告知办公室。

3. 回到短信息，匹配选项

   音乐会门票通知：在学校网站上购买，然后到办公室领取。A选项与通知相符，pay for是buy的同义转换，pick up是collect的同义转换。B选项和C选项未提及。故正确答案是A。

Day 4　信息匹配题

 题型分析

【题型】信息匹配题，单选，三选一

【题量】7题

【内容】同一主题的3个短文和7个问题

【要求】将每个问题与其中一个短文相匹配

【样例】

Part 2

Questions 7 – 13

For each question, choose the correct answer.

		Amy	Flora	Louisa
7	Whose class learnt about the garden competition from a TV programme?	A	B	C
8	Whose class grew some vegetables?	A	B	C
9	Whose class won a trip in the school garden competition?	A	B	C
10	Whose class painted flowers on their garden wall?	A	B	C
11	Whose class learnt about the insects in their garden?	A	B	C
12	Whose class got help from someone in a pupil's family?	A	B	C
13	Whose class chose flowers that were the same colour?	A	B	C

School gardens competition

 Amy

Our class has just won a prize for our school garden in a competition – and they're going to make a TV film about it! The judges liked our garden because the flowers are all different colours – and we painted some more on the wall around it. My cousin gave us advice about what to grow – she's learning about gardening at college. We're planning to grow some vegetables next year. I just hope the insects don't eat them all!

 Flora

Our teacher heard about the school garden competition on TV and told us about it. We decided to enter and won second prize! There's a high wall in our garden where many red and yellow climbing flowers grow and it looks as pretty as a painting! Our prize is a visit to a special garden where there are lots of butterflies and other insects. My aunt works there and she says it's amazing.

 Louisa

The garden our class entered in the competition is very special. The flowers we've grown are all yellow! They look lovely on the video we made of the garden. We also grew lots of carrots and potatoes, and everyone says they taste fantastic. It was an interesting project. Our teacher taught us lots of things about the butterflies in our garden. We also watched a TV programme about them, and did some paintings to put on the classroom wall.

 答题技巧

核心考点

　✓　考查考生快速阅读和提取特定关键信息的能力。

答题步骤与建议

　1. 考生应先仔细阅读问题，找出关键信息，然后再快速浏览原文，找出哪篇文章有你需要的答案。

　2. 有些问题的关键信息在文中会被替换成有相同、相近意思或否定、相反意思的表达。

　3. 看见不懂的单词可以联合上下文进行解读。

　4. 问题的排列顺序与原文信息的排列顺序并不相同。

样题解析

For each question, choose the correct answer.

		Amy	Flora	Louisa
7	Whose class learnt about the garden competition from a TV programme?	A	B	C
8	Whose class grew some vegetables?	A	B	C
9	Whose class won a trip in the school garden competition?	A	B	C
10	Whose class painted flowers on their garden wall?	A	B	C
11	Whose class learnt about the insects in their garden?	A	B	C
12	Whose class got help from someone in a pupil's family?	A	B	C
13	Whose class chose flowers that were the same colour?	A	B	C

School gardens competition

Amy

Our class has just won a prize for our school garden in a competition – and they're going to make a TV film about it! The judges liked our garden because the flowers are all different colours – and we painted some more on the wall around it. My cousin gave us advice about what to grow – she's learning about gardening at college. We're planning to grow some vegetables next year. I just hope the insects don't eat them all!

Flora

Our teacher heard about the school garden competition on TV and told us about it. We decided to enter and won second prize! There's a high wall in our garden where many red and yellow climbing flowers grow and it looks as pretty as a painting! Our prize is a visit to a special garden where there are lots of butterflies and other insects. My aunt works there and she says it's amazing.

Louisa

The garden our class entered in the competition is very special. The flowers we've grown are all yellow! They look lovely on the video we made of the garden. We also grew lots of carrots and potatoes, and everyone says they taste fantastic. It was an interesting project. Our teacher taught us lots of things about the butterflies in our garden. We also watched a TV programme about them, and did some paintings to put on the classroom wall.

解析

Step 1:【审题目，划重点】

7. [题干] Whose class learnt about **the garden competition from a TV programme**? 谁的班从电视节目中了解到园艺比赛？

8. [题干] Whose class **grew some vegetables**? 谁的班种了一些蔬菜？

9. [题干] Whose class **won a trip** in the school garden competition? 谁的班在学校园艺比赛中赢得了一次旅行？

10. [题干] Whose class **painted flowers on their garden wall**? 谁的班在花园墙上画了花？

11. [题干] Whose class **learnt about the insects** in their garden? 谁的班在他们的花园里学习了昆虫？

12. [题干] Whose class **got help from someone in a pupil's family**? 谁的班得到了学生家人的帮助？

13. [题干] Whose class **chose flowers that were the same colour**? 谁的班选了相同颜色的花？

Step 2:【找线索，选答案】

7. 注意题干中的关键词TV programme，三个人物介绍中只有Flora提到Our teacher heard about the school garden competition on TV（我们老师从电视上听到了学校园艺比赛的消息），原文中的heard about和题干中的learnt about同义。由此得知，本题应选B。

8. 根据文章信息，Louisa在介绍学校园艺比赛时提到We also grew lots of carrots and potatoes（我们还种了很多胡萝卜和土豆），原文中的carrots and potatoes和题干中的vegetables是所属关系，胡萝卜和土豆属于蔬菜，故本题选C。

9. 注意题干中的关键词won a trip，三个人物介绍中只有Flora提到Our prize is a visit to a special garden where there are lots of butterflies and other insects.（我们的奖品是参观一个特殊的花园，那里有很多蝴蝶和其他昆虫。）原文中的a visit和题干中的a trip意思相近，由此得知，本题应选B。

10. 文章中Amy在描述时，提到The judges liked our garden because the flowers are all different colours – and we painted some more on the wall around it.（评委们很喜欢我们的花园，因为花都是不同的颜色——我们在周围的墙上又画了一些。）由此可知，Amy班在花园墙上画了花，故选A。

11. Louisa在介绍时提到，Our teacher taught us lots of things about the butterflies in our garden.（我们的老师在花园里教了我们很多关于蝴蝶的知识。）原文中的our teacher taught us和whose class learnt about是同义转换，且句中the butterflies和题干中的the insects是所属关系，蝴蝶是昆虫的一种，故正确答案是C。

12. 根据题干中的关键词a pupil's family可以定位到原文中Amy和Flora的描述。文章中Amy提到My cousin gave us advice about what to grow – she's learning about gardening at college.（我的表姐给了我们关于种植什么的建议——她正在大学里学习园艺。）原文中的gave us advice是题干中got help的同义转换，故选A。Flora的描述中提到My aunt works there and she says it's amazing.（我阿姨在那里工作，她说那里很棒。）句中并未提及获得任何帮助，故选项B排除。正确答案是A。

13. 根据文章信息，关于花的颜色，文章中Amy提到the flowers are all different colours（花都是不同的颜色），故排除。Flora提到There's a high wall in our garden where many red and yellow climbing flowers grow（我们的花园有一堵高墙，墙上长着许多红色和黄色的攀缘花），花有红色和黄色，所以花的颜色不同，故排除。Louisa在介绍花园时提到，The flowers we've grown are all yellow!（我们种的花都是黄色的！）所以Louisa班级的花颜色相同，符合题干中的the same colour，故正确答案选C。

【Answer key】

7. B	8. C	9. B	10. A	11. C	12. A	13. C

Week 1

Day 5 　阅读理解题

 题型分析

【题型】阅读理解题，单选，三选一

【题量】5题

【内容】一篇长文章，来源于报纸或杂志等；共有5道选择题，每道题各有3个选项

【要求】阅读一篇长文章，完成5道选择题

【样例】

Part 3

Questions 14 – 18

For each question, choose the correct answer.

Starting at a new school

By Anna Gray, age 11

I've just finished my first week at a new school and I'd like to tell you about it. Like other children in my country, I went to primary school until I was eleven and then I had to go to a different school for older children. I loved my primary school but I was excited to move to a new school.

It was very strange on our first day. There were some kids from my primary school there, but most of the children in my year group were from different schools. But I soon started talking to the girl who was sitting beside me in maths. She lives near me so we walked home together. We're best friends now.

When I saw our timetable there were lots of subjects, some were quite new to me! Lessons are harder now. They're longer and the subjects are more difficult, but the teachers help us a lot.

At primary school we had all our lessons in one classroom. Now each subject is taught in a different room. It was difficult to find the classrooms at first because the school is so big. But the teachers gave us each a map of the school, so it's getting easier now.

The worst thing is that I have lots more homework to do now. Some of it is fun but I need to get better at remembering when I have to give different pieces of work to the teachers!

14　How did Anna feel about moving to a new school?

　A　worried about being with lots of older children

　B　happy about the idea of doing something different

　C　pleased because she was bored at her primary school

15　Who has become Anna's best friend at her new school?

　A　someone from her primary school

　B　someone she knew from her home area

　C　someone she met in her new class

16　What does Anna say about the timetable at her new school?

　A　It includes subjects she didn't do at primary school.

　B　She has shorter lessons than she had at her old school.

　C　It is quite difficult to understand.

17　Why couldn't Anna find her classrooms?

　A　She couldn't read a map.

　B　There was little time between lessons.

　C　The school building was very large.

18　What does Anna say about the homework she has now?

　A　She gets more help from some teachers than others.

　B　She thinks it is the hardest part of school life.

　C　She remembers everything she's told to do.

 答题技巧

核心考点

　✓ 考查考生对较长文章的主旨理解，以及抓取细节信息的能力。

答题步骤及建议

　1. 考生应略读文章，快速阅读各段首句，理解文章的主旨和大意。

　2. 快速浏览每道题目题干及选项信息，初步了解答题关键点。

　3. 回到原文中，定位段落和句子，找到最匹配的一项。

4. 选定答案后，应检查其他两个选项，知道错误的选项错在哪里，以作检查验证。

 样题解析

PART 3

QUESTIONS 14-18

For each question, choose the correct answer.

Starting at a new school

By Anna Gray, age 11

I've just finished my first week at a new school and I'd like to tell you about it. Like other children in my country, I went to primary school until I was eleven and then I had to go to a different school for older children. I loved my primary school but I was excited to move to a new school.

It was very strange on our first day. There were some kids from my primary school there, but most of the children in my year group were from different schools. But I soon started talking to the girl who was sitting beside me in maths. She lives near me so we walked home together. We're best friends now.

When I saw our timetable there were lots of subjects, some were quite new to me! Lessons are harder now. They're longer and the subjects are more difficult, but the teachers help us a lot.

At primary school we had all our lessons in one classroom. Now each subject is taught in a different room. It was difficult to find the classrooms at first because the school is so big. But the teachers gave us each a map of the school, so it's getting easier now.

The worst thing is that I have lots more homework to do now. Some of it is fun but I need to get better at remembering when I have to give different pieces of work to the teachers!

---

14 How did Anna feel about moving to a new school?

   A worried about being with lots of older children

B happy about the idea of doing something different

C pleased because she was bored at her primary school

15 Who has become Anna's best friend at her new school?

A someone from her primary school

B someone she knew from her home area

C someone she met in her new class

16 What does Anna say about the timetable at her new school?

A It includes subjects she didn't do at primary school.

B She has shorter lessons than she had at her old school.

C It is quite difficult to understand.

17 Why couldn't Anna find her classrooms?

A She couldn't read a map.

B There was little time between lessons.

C The school building was very large.

18 What does Anna say about the homework she has now?

A She gets more help from some teachers than others.

B She thinks it is the hardest part of school life.

C She remembers everything she's told to do.

解析

Step 1:【审题目，划重点】

14. [题干] **How** did Anna **feel** about moving to a new school? 安娜对搬到一所新学校有什么感觉?

A选项，worried about being with lots of older children（担心和很多大孩子在一起）；B选项，happy about the idea of doing something different（做点不一样的事情很开心）；C选项，pleased because she was bored at her primary school（很高兴，因为她在小学很无聊）

15. [题干] **Who** has become **Anna's best friend** at her new school? 谁成了安娜在新学校最好的朋友?

A选项，someone from her primary school（她小学的同学）；B选项，someone

she knew from her home area（她在家乡认识的人）；C选项，someone she met in her new class（她在新班里遇到的人）

16. [题干] What does Anna say about **the timetable** at her new school? 安娜对她新学校的课程表有什么看法？

    A选项，It includes subjects she didn't do at primary school.（它包括她在小学没有学过的科目。）B选项，She has shorter lessons than she had at her old school.（她上的课比她在旧学校的课短。）C选项，It is quite difficult to understand.（很难理解。）

17. [题干] Why **couldn't** Anna **find** her **classrooms**?（为什么安娜找不到她的教室？）

    A选项，She couldn't read a map.（她看不懂地图。）B选项，There was little time between lessons.（课间的时间很少。）C选项，The school building was very large.（教学楼非常大。）

18. [题干] What does Anna say about **the homework** she has now? 关于现在的家庭作业，安娜说了什么？

    A选项，She gets more help from some teachers than others.（她从一些老师那里得到的帮助比其他老师多。）B选项，She thinks it is the hardest part of school life.（她认为这是学校生活中最难的部分。）C选项，She remembers everything she's told to do.（她能记住所有让她做的事。）

Step 2:【回原文，找答案】

14. 文章第一段最后一句话提到，I loved my primary school but I was excited to move to a new school.（我喜欢我的小学，但我很兴奋能搬到一所新学校。）原文中的excited与题干中的happy意思相近，原文中的go to a different school等同于doing something different，由此可知本题选B。根据文章第一段的内容，安娜对去新学校感到excited，而不是worried；她喜欢（loved）自己的小学，未提及bored，故排除A、C。

15. 文章第二段中第三句和最后一句提到，But I soon started talking to the girl who was sitting beside me in maths.（但我很快就开始和数学课上坐在我旁边的女孩聊天了。）We're best friends now.（我们现在是最好的朋友了。）原文中sitting beside me in maths等同于C选项中met in her new class，故选C。第二句

提到"那里有一些来自我小学的孩子，但我所在年级的大多数孩子来自不同的学校"，故A和B可排除。本题正确答案为C。

16. 根据题干中的the timetable可定位到文章第三段。第一句提到，When I saw our timetable there were lots of subjects, some were quite new to me! Lessons are harder now.（当我看到我们的时间表时，上面有很多科目，有些对我来说是全新的！现在课程更难了。）原文中的quite new与题干中的didn't do at primary school意思相近，故选A。最后一句提到，"现在的课程更长，科目更难，但老师帮了我们很多"，故B和C可排除。所以本题正确答案为A。

17. 文章第四段第三句提到，It was difficult to find the classrooms at first because the school is so big.（起初很难找到教室，因为学校太大了。）原文中的so big等于题干中的very large，故选C。最后一句提到，"但是老师们给了我们每人一张学校的地图，所以现在变得越来越容易了"，A和B文中未提及，所以本题正确答案为C。

18. 根据文章最后一段第一句，The worst thing is that I have lots more homework to do now.（最糟糕的是我现在有更多的家庭作业要做。）原文中the worst thing等于题干中的the hardest part，故选B。

【Answer key】

14. B   15. C   16. A   17. C   18. B

Day 6 完形填空题

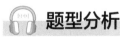

题型分析

【题型】完形填空，单选，三选一

【题量】6题

【内容】一篇短文，文章中留有6个空，每道题有三个文本选项

【要求】阅读一篇事实类的短文，选择恰当的选项

【样例】

Questions 19 – 24   Part 4

For each question, choose the correct answer.

Wivenhoe hotel

Wivenhoe is a beautiful hotel in the countryside, with many rooms and an excellent restaurant. However, there is a big (19) ....between Wivenhoe and other hotels. Firstly, Wivenhoe is part of a university, and secondly, its staff are all teenagers.

In fact, Wivenhoe is a hotel school for young people who are (20) ....to get jobs in the hotel or restaurant (21)................. The students learn by helping staff in a real hotel, while their teachers (22)................them carefully. They do everything, from making beds and cleaning bathrooms to preparing menus and (23)................ the telephone.

Some British people may think that a hotel run by students is a rather strange idea, but many visitors say that Wivenhoe is the best hotel they have ever (24)............... at.

19	A	change	B	variety	C	difference
20	A	knowing	B	hoping	C	explaining
21	A	business	B	work	C	career
22	A	see	B	look	C	watch
23	A	calling	B	answering	C	speaking
24	A	entered	B	stayed	C	gone

 ## 答题技巧

核心考点

✓ 考查考生在语境中辨析词语的能力。

✓ 题目考查的重点是词汇，但也会测试少量的语法。

答题步骤及建议

1. 考生应先略读文章，理解文章的主旨和大意。

2. 仔细阅读空格所在的句子，在3个选项中，选择恰当的词。

3. 答完题后，再通读一遍全文，确保文章意思合理、通顺。

 ## 样题解析

For each question, choose the correct answer.

Wivenhoe hotel

Wivenhoe is a beautiful hotel in the countryside, with many rooms and an excellent restaurant. However, there is a big (19) _____ between Wivenhoe and other hotels. Firstly, Wivenhoe is part of a university, and secondly, its staff are all teenagers.

In fact, Wivenhoe is a hotel school for young people who are (20) _____ to get jobs in the hotel or restaurant (21) _____. The students learn by helping staff in a real hotel, while their teachers (22) _____ them carefully. They do everything, from making beds and cleaning bathrooms to preparing menus and (23) _____ the telephone.

Some British people may think that a hotel run by students is a rather strange idea, but many visitors say that Wivenhoe is the best hotel they have ever (24) _____ at.

19 A change	B variety	C difference
20 A knowing	B hoping	C explaining
21 A business	B work	C career
22 A see	B look	C watch
23 A calling	B answering	C speaking
24 A entered	B stayed	C gone

解析

Step 1:【读文章，知大意】

　　1. 文章主旨

　　　　这篇文章主要介绍了Wivenhoe酒店，它是一所位于乡村的美丽酒店，拥有许多客房和一家优秀的餐厅，且其独特之处在于它是大学的一部分，员工都是青少年。

　　2. 考点　考查名词辨析和动词辨析。

Step 2:【找线索，选答案】

19. C

【考点】名词辨析

【解析】A选项change意为"变化"，B选项variety意为"多样"，C选项difference意为"不同"。关键词为空格后的between... and...。difference between A and B为固定搭配，表示"A和B之间的差别"，句意为"然而，Wivenhoe酒店和其他酒店有很大的不同。"故选C。

20. B

【考点】动词辨析

【解析】A选项knowing意为"知道"，B选项hoping意为"希望"，C选项explaining意为"解释"。关键词为空格后的to，选项中只有hope后面加to do，hope to do sth. 表示"希望做某事"。故选B。

21. A

【考点】名词辨析

【解析】A选项business意为"行业"，B选项work意为"工作"，C选项career意为"事业"。根据句意"事实上，Wivenhoe是一所酒店学校，面向希望在酒店或餐饮业找到工作的年轻人。"可知空格处应填表示"行业"的词。hotel or restaurant business表示"酒店行业或餐饮业"。故选A。

22. C

【考点】动词辨析

【解析】A选项see意为"看见"，强调看的结果。B选项look意为"看"，后面加宾语时要加介词at，常用短语为look at，意为"看"，空格后无at，故排除B。C选项watch意为"看，观察"，常用于看电视、看比赛，一般指仔细观察。watch them carefully表示"仔细看"，句意为"学生们在真正的酒店里通过帮助工作人员来学习，而他们的老师则仔细观察他们。"故选C。

23. B

【考点】动词辨析

【解析】A选项calling意为"（给……）打电话"，B选项answering意为"回答"，C选项speaking意为"说"。关键词为空格后的the telephone，answer the phone / telephone为固定搭配，意为"接电话"。句意为"他们什么都做，从铺床、打扫浴室到准备菜单和接电话。"故选B。

24. B

【考点】动词辨析

【解析】A选项entered意为"进入"，B选项stayed意为"待过"，C选项gone意为"离开"。关键词为空格后的at，enter后直接加地点，go后面加介词to再加地点。根据句意"一些英国人可能认为由学生经营的酒店是一个相当奇怪的想法，但许多游客说，Wivenhoe是他们住过的最好的酒店。"可知stayed符合，即stayed at the hotel。故选B。

【Answer key】

| 19. C | 20. B | 21. A | 22. C | 23. B | 24. B |

Day 7 语法填空题

 题型分析

【题型】语法填空题

【题量】6题

【内容】1～2篇电子邮件，文章中留有6个空，每空一词

【要求】拼写正确，每小题填一个单词

【样例】

Part 5

Questions 25 – 30

For each question, write the correct answer.
Write **one** word for each gap.

Example: | 0 | for |

From:	Anita
To:	Sasha

Thank you **(0)** .... your email. Living in Canada sounds really great! I'm glad that you like **(25)** .... new house. What's the weather like? **(26)** .... it very cold in Canada? Does it snow every day?

I heard that a **(27)** .... of Canadians speak two languages – English <u>and</u> French. Are you having French lessons? Do you watch programmes **(28)** .... TV in French too?

How about the students in your new school? Are **(29)** .... friendly? And send some photos too – I would like to know more about them.

I've got **(30)** .... go now, but I'll write again soon.

 答题技巧

核心考点

✓ 考查考生邮件阅读理解、语法应用的能力。

✓ 题目主要考查两位说话者的观点、态度、意见等。

答题步骤与建议

1. 考生应先略读文章，找出文章的主旨和大意。

2. 仔细阅读空格处所在的句子，找出答题关键词。

3. 单词拼写正确，句子首字母一定要大写。

4. 填写完后通读一遍，看文章是否通顺。

🎧 样题解析

For each question, write the correct answer.

Write one word for each gap.

Example:	**0**	for

From:	Anita
To:	Sasha

Thank you **(0)** _____ your email. Living in Canada sounds really great! I'm glad that you like **(25)** _____ new house. What's the weather like? **(26)** _____ it very cold in Canada? Does it snow every day?

I heard that a **(27)** _____ of Canadians speak two languages—English and French. Are you having French lessons? Do you watch programmes **(28)** _____ TV in French too?

How about the students in your new school? Are **(29)** _____ friendly? And send some photos too — I would like to know more about them.

I've got **(30)** _____ go now, but I'll write again soon.

解析

Step 1:【读文章，知大意】

1. 文章主旨

这是一篇Anita回复Sasha的邮件，表达了她对加拿大生活的兴趣，并询问了加拿大的天气、语言学习以及新学校的情况，并请求发来照片。

2. 考点　考查冠词、代词、介词、be动词和固定搭配。

Step 2:【找线索，填答案】

25. your / the

【考点】冠词或代词

【解析】根据句意"很高兴你喜欢新房子"，house为名词，可以用冠词the或形容词性物主代词your修饰。故正确答案为your或the。

26. Is

【考点】be动词

【解析】根据问号可知，本句为疑问句。根据句意"在加拿大非常冷吗？"可知本句为一般疑问句，主语为it，是第三人称单数，时态为一般现在时，be动词要用is。单词位于句首，首字母大写。故正确答案为Is。

27. lot

【考点】固定搭配

【解析】关键词Canadians（加拿大人）为可数名词复数。根据前后内容，可知此处考查短语"a lot of（许多的）+可数名词复数"，句意为"我听说许多加拿大人说两种语言——英语和法语"。故正确答案为lot。

28. on

【考点】介词

【解析】句意为"你也在电视上看法语节目吗？"表示"在电视上"用介词on。故正确答案为on。

29. they

【考点】代词

【解析】本句为are引导的一般疑问句，句子为主系表结构，are为系动词，表语为形容词friendly（友好的），故本题缺少主语。结合前句提到"你的新学校的同学们怎么样？"可知本句句意为"他们友好吗？"所以，此处应填人称代词主格形式they（他们）。

30. to

【考点】固定搭配

【解析】本题考查固定短语have got to do sth.（必须做某事）。此处句意为"我现在必须走了，但是我很快将会再次写信给你"。故正确答案为to。

【 Answer key 】

| 25. your / the | 26. Is | 27. lot | 28. on | 29. they | 30. to |

Week 2　阅读通关技巧

Day 1　基础备考技巧

考点汇总

A2 Key考试阅读部分使用的文本改编自真实的阅读文本。阅读材料来源包括通知、标识、包装信息、便条、电子邮件、卡片、短信、报纸、杂志、小册子、传单、网站、简化百科全书、其他非小说类书籍。阅读各部分的文章词数不同，整体词数在10～270之间。

Part	材料来源	词数
Part 1 短信息选择题	通知、标识、包装信息、便条、电子邮件、卡片、短信	10～30
Part 2 信息匹配题	报纸、杂志、小册子、传单、网站	230～270
Part 3 阅读理解题	报纸、杂志、小册子、传单、网站	240～270
Part 4 完形填空题	报纸、杂志、简化百科全书、其他非小说类书籍、网站	120～140
Part 5 语法填空题	便条、电子邮件、卡片、短信	80～110

阅读部分考查主题与A2 Key官方手册主题高度吻合，包括日常生活、购物、休闲娱乐、学校学习、体育运动、度假旅行、人物介绍等。阅读部分考查知识点主要有同义替换、词汇辨析、语法辨析等。

Part	考查主题	考查知识点
Part 1 短信息选择题	学校学习、日常生活、休闲娱乐、度假旅行等	同义替换、信息识别
Part 2 信息匹配题	人物介绍、度假旅行、休闲娱乐等	同义替换、信息匹配
Part 3 阅读理解题	人物经历、度假旅行、休闲娱乐等	同义替换、细节区分
Part 4 完形填空题	名人介绍、度假旅行、知识科普等	名词辨析、动词辨析、形容词辨析、副词辨析、限定词辨析
Part 5 语法填空题	假期游玩、班级活动、特殊节日、聚会邀请、体育运动等	冠词、代词、介词、连词、比较级、动词、固定搭配、句型等

 解题关键

答题通用步骤

审题 ➡ 作答 ➡ 检查

1. 审题
   ✓ 审题目说明——了解事件、场景等背景信息。
   ✓ 审题干——了解出题点及核心考查内容，划重点。
   ✓ 审选项——熟悉选项内容，画出关键信息。
   ✓ 定位——快速定位到答案段落，在原文中找匹配。

2. 作答
   ✓ 选择/填入正确答案。

3. 检查
   ✓ 填写完后通读一遍，看文章是否通顺。
   ✓ 检查单词拼写是否正确。

以上三步完成后，最后将答案誊写到答题卡中。

答题阅读方法

在A2 Key考试中，需要掌握扫读和精读两种阅读方法。

扫读 ➡ 精读

1. 扫读：一种快速阅读方法，目的是快速找到所需信息。

   ✓ 扫读时，读文章的主旨句，即首句或末句，以便快速理解文章的主旨和要点。

   ✓ 读有转折关系的连接词、有主观色彩的形容词和副词所在句，可能会是出题点。

   ✓ 扫读过程中如果遇到生词或不认识的表达，不要纠结，直接跳过。

   ✓ 略过不重要的细节来提高阅读速度。

2. 精读：一种更深入的阅读方法，需要仔细阅读文章并理解其细节和深层含义。

   ✓ 注意细节——注意文章中的细节，包括单词、短语、语法和表达方式等。考生需要认真阅读，逐句分析，注意语言的使用和含义。

   ✓ 查阅字典——在精读时，可能会遇到一些生词、短语或概念，需要查阅字典或参考资料来理解。

   ✓ 做笔记——在精读时，可以边读边做笔记，记录下重要的信息、细节和语言点。

   ✓ 反复阅读和练习——精读需要反复进行，不断练习和提高。考生可以通过反复阅读同一篇文章或相似文章来巩固记忆和理解，同时也可以通过练习题来检验自己的掌握程度。

在A2 Key考试中，根据实际情况选择适当的阅读方法很重要。如果时间紧张，可以选择扫读法快速找到所需信息；如果时间充足，可以选择精读法深入理解文章内容。结合扫读和精读两种方法，能更好地应对不同类型的阅读题和考试要求。

Day 2 训练同义替换反应能力

 考点重现

阅读考试中，同义替换是重要考点之一，包括近义词替换、反词义替换、抽象到具体替换和英英释义替换，现将曾考过的部分内容汇总如下。

同义替换	
考点	**真题举例**
近义词替换	hard 困难的 / difficult 困难的
	excited 激动的 / happy 高兴的
	so big 如此大 / very large 非常大
	hear about 听说 / learn about 听说
	a visit 一次参观 / a trip 一次旅行
	the worst thing 最糟糕的事 / the hardest part 最糟糕的部分
	giving advice 给建议 / answers questions 回答问题
	gave us advice 给我们建议 / got help 获得帮助
	give ballet lessons 上芭蕾舞课 / teach ballet lessons 教芭蕾舞课
	our teacher taught us 我们的老师教我们 / our class learnt about 我们的班学到了
反义词替换	come to school as normal 照常到校上课 / cannot have a day off school 不能放一天假
	almost nobody 几乎没有人 / didn't have many people 没有很多人
抽象到具体替换	vegetables 蔬菜 / carrots and potatoes 胡萝卜和土豆
	my cousin 我表姐 / a member of her family 她的家庭成员
	college magazine 大学杂志 / other types of writing 其他写作类型
	the same colour 相同的颜色 / all yellow 都是黄色的
英英释义替换	as soon as she could walk 当她能走路的时候 / at a very young age 在很小的时候
	sitting beside me in maths 数学课上坐在我旁边 / met in her new class 在她的新班里认识的
	go to a different school 去一所不同的学校 / doing something different 尝试做一些不同的事情
	buy these on the school website 在学校网站上购买 / pay for tickets online 网上购票
	picking them up at school 到学校领取 / collect them from the office 去办公室取票
	what the maths homework is 数学作业是什么 / what we have to do before Thursday's maths class 在星期四的数学课之前我们要做什么

🎧 考点锦囊

1. 不同的单词可以表达同一个意思或者在一定语境下可以同义替换。关于常考的近义词替换总结如下。

近义词替换	
friendly 友好的	nice 友好的
pleased 高兴的	glad 高兴的
famous 著名的	well-known 众所周知的
good 好的	great 好的
hard 困难的	difficult 困难的
sport 运动	exercise 运动
flat 公寓	apartment 公寓
laptop 笔记本电脑	computer 电脑
favourite 最喜欢的	like... most / best 最喜欢
everyone 每个人	each person 每个人
cycle 骑自行车	by bike 骑自行车
return 归还	give back 归还
walk 步行	on foot 步行
photography 摄影	taking pictures 拍照
prepare 准备	get ready to 准备好
go to the cinema 看电影	see a film 看电影
no longer 不再	not... anymore 不再
half price 半价	50% off / discount 五折
be quiet 保持安静	don't make any noise 不要喧哗
crowded 拥挤的	busy road 繁忙的公路
a variety of 各种各样的	different kinds of 不同种类的
be careful 小心	look out 小心，当心
a year ago 一年前	twelve months ago 十二个月前

2. 反义词替换，其实就是"反着说"，比如"昂贵的"替换"不便宜"，此类替换难度不大，但是又需要一定的理解能力。反义词替换经常出现在信息匹配题和阅读理解题中。关于常考的反义词替换总结如下。

反义词替换	
surprised 惊讶的	couldn't believe 不相信
expensive 昂贵的	not cheap 不便宜
boring 无聊的	not very interesting 不是很有趣
hard 困难的	not easy 不容易
danger 危险的	unsafe 不安全
too small 太小	not big enough 不够大
too dark 很黑	not bright enough 不够亮
sold out 售罄	no tickets left 没有票了
on sale 打折	cost less than usual 花费比平时少
free of charge 免费	don't have to pay 不用付钱
remember to do 记得做	don't forget 不要忘记

3. 抽象到具体替换，是指将抽象、概括性的表述或词汇替换为更具体、详细的表述或词汇，两者通常是所属关系，比如"水果"替换"橘子"。关于常考的抽象到具体替换总结如下。

抽象到具体替换	
fruit 水果	oranges 橘子；grapes 葡萄
food 食物	snacks 小吃；sandwich 三明治
drink 饮料	juice 果汁；milk 牛奶
family 家人	mother 妈妈；aunt 阿姨；uncle 叔叔
hobby 爱好	swimming 游泳；drawing 画画
sports 运动	run 跑步；basketball 篮球
sports equipment 运动器材	ball 球；bat 球拍
art equipment 美术用具	pencil 铅笔；paint 颜料

4. 英英释义替换，是指用英文解释来替换文章中的某个词汇或短语，比如"weekends（周末）"替换为"Saturdays and Sundays（星期六和星期日）"。关于常考的英英释义替换总结如下。

英英释义替换	
weekdays 工作日	from Monday to Friday 从星期一至星期五
weekends 周末	Saturdays and Sundays 星期六和星期日
swimming 游泳	spend time at the pool 在游泳池消磨时间
sailing 航行	go out on a boat 坐船出去
juice 果汁	something to drink 一些喝的东西
bread 面包	something to eat 一些吃的东西
library 图书馆	a place to borrow books 借书的地方
scarf 围巾	keep warm in winter 在冬天保暖
neighbour 邻居	the person who lives next door 住在隔壁的人
photo 照片	something to put on the bedroom wall 放在卧室墙上的东西
hall 大厅	the entrance by the front door 前门的入口
farm 农场	an area of land for growing crops 种植庄稼的土地
backpack 背包	put the school books in it 把课本放进去

🎧 百变演练

Match the words in the box to the descriptions. 根据下面的句子匹配框中的单词。

flower	bus	doctor	sister	cake	apple

1. a sweet juicy fruit that grows on trees   _____

2. whose job is to treat people who are ill   _____

3. a vehicle that carries passengers   _____

4. a girl who has the same mother with you   _____

5. a sweet food   _____

6. a part of a plant which is often brightly coloured   _____

Day 3 提升词汇辨识能力

 考点重现

　　阅读考试中，意思相近的词作为选项让考生辨别是重要考点之一，包括名词、动词、形容词、副词等，现将曾考过的部分词汇总如下。

类别	真题举例		
名词	business 生意	career 事业	occupation 职业
	business 行业	work 工作	career 事业
	change 变化	variety 多样	difference 不同
	class 班级	subject 科目	course 课程
	day 天	time 时间	hour 小时
	kinds 种类	ways 方法	things 事情
	way 方法	path 小路	plan 计划
动词	began 开始	arrived 到达	became 开始变得
	borrows 借用	lends 借给	belongs 属于
	brought 带来	turned 变成	opened 开业
	calling 打电话	answering 回答	speaking 说
	comes 来	begins 开始	starts 开始
	describe 描述	explain 解释	discuss 讨论
	done 做	used 用	got 获得
	entered 进入	stayed 待	gone 去，走
	filled 装满	carried 拿；搬	collected 收集
	keeps 保持	belongs 属于	lends 借
	knowing 知道	hoping 希望	explaining 解释
	leave 离开	miss 错过	lose 丢失
	made 使，让	put 放；安置	added 加起来
	paid 付款	bought 买	spent 花费
	planned 计划	decided 决定	preferred 更喜欢
	plays 播放	puts 放	sends 发送

类别	真题举例		
动词	prefer 更喜欢	think 认为	decide 决定
	see 看见	look 看	watch 观察
	standing 站立	thinking 认为	waiting 等待
	thinking 认为	trying 试图	deciding 决定
	visit 拜访	go 去	arrive 到达
形容词	high 高的	full 满的	large 大的
	large 大的	far 较远的	long 长的
	tall 有……高	long 长	large 大的
	wonderful 精彩的	important 重要的	advanced 先进的
副词	especially 尤其	however 然而	instead 反而
	immediately 立即	suddenly 突然	actually 事实上
限定词	lots 大量	much 很多	several 一些

🎧 考点锦囊

1. 名词辨析主要涉及比较和辨识不同名词之间的含义和用法，以确保在特定语境中能够正确、恰当地使用。比如，problem和question都有"问题"的意思，但problem多跟solve连用，question多跟answer连用，具体含义和使用场景不同，需要仔细辨别。关于常考的名词辨析总结如下。

teenager和youth都表示"年轻人、青少年"	
teenager	主要指13岁到19岁之间的青少年，强调这个年龄段孩子本身的特点
youth	泛指"青年"，即介于小孩和成年之间的年轻人，有时youth专指男青年
problem和question都表示"问题"	
problem	通常指遇到的需要处理并且等待解决的问题，多和slove搭配
question	多指等待答复或需要进行思考才能得到答案的问题，比如，answer the question（回答问题）
exercise和practice都表示"练习、锻炼"	
exercise	指适用于正常人的一般性的以健身为目的的体质锻炼，也可指脑力方面的锻炼
practice	指把所学的理论或知识用于实践以获得技艺与技巧

method、way和means都表示"方法、方式"	
method	指在做某项工作或为达到某目的时所采取的有系统、有条理地办事或解决问题的方法
way	是普通用词，可指一般的方法，也可指特殊的方式或方法
means	指为达到某种目的或目标而采用的方法、手段或途径
child和baby都表示"孩子"	
child	是普通用词，含义广，无感情色彩。一般指从2岁至14岁的孩子，不分男孩女孩
baby	是日常用词，一般指还不会说话或走路的婴儿（0~2岁），常含感情色彩
cap和hat都表示"帽子"	
cap	可指无边的便帽，也可指制服帽，比如，a baseball cap（棒球帽）
hat	指周边有檐的帽子，比如，straw hat（草帽）
clothes和clothing都表示"衣服、服装"	
clothes	是普通用词，多指具体的衣服，比如，上衣、内衣或裤子等
clothing	是常用词，集合名词，是衣服的总称
dinner和meal都表示"餐"	
dinner	意为"正餐"，指一天中的主餐，英语国家一天最为丰盛的一餐常为晚餐，因此dinner常指晚餐
meal	泛指一日三餐的任一餐，也可指一餐所吃的东西，为可数名词，"一日三餐"可用three meals a day来表达
plate和dish都表示"盘子"	
plate	指供个人分菜食用的盘子，也可表示上食物或用来吃食物的浅盘子
dish	是"盘子"的总称，如"洗碗"可用do the dishes来表达
armchair、chair和bench都表示"椅子"	
armchair	指有扶手的椅子，比如，massage chair（按摩椅）
chair	指有靠背，有时还指有扶手的单人椅
bench	指可供两人或更多人坐的长凳或石凳，一般为木制或石制，多置于公园中
door和gate都表示"门"	
door	通常指楼、房间、碗橱、壁橱等建筑物或家具上的门，一般有墙有顶
gate	一般指比较大的门，如校园、公园、工厂、城市或庭院等的大门
home、family和house都表示"家"	
home	主要指一个人出生或居住的地方，房屋是其中的一部分，因而也有"家乡、故乡"的意思，含感情色彩

family	指构成一个家庭的全体成员，当它作为整体概念的"家庭"讲时是单数，当"家庭成员"讲时是复数，与家里的房子无关
house	一般指家人所居住的建筑物，不带感情色彩
tool和equipment都表示"仪器、设备、器具"	
tool	一般指能使操作更为方便的工具，尤指用手工操作的工具（如刨、锯等），是可数名词
equipment	多指成套的或重型的全套设备，如装备、器械、仪表等。通常用作不可数名词
costume、uniform和suit都表示"服装"	
costume	指某地或某历史时期的服装，也可指演员的戏装
uniform	指制服，如军服、校服等
suit	指用同一料子做成的一套服装，一般指含短上衣、裤子或裙子的套装

2. 动词辨析是对一些含义或用法相似的动词进行比较和分析，以确定在特定语境中的使用。动词辨析包括动词的基本含义和用法辨析。关于常考的动词辨析总结如下。

watch和look都表示"看"	
watch	指用眼睛跟踪某物以观察到每一个动作、变化、危险迹象、机会等
look	强调看的动作
hear和listen都表示"听"	
hear	强调听的结果。是及物动词，后面可以直接跟名词，比如，She heard footsteps behind her.（她听到背后有脚步声。）
listen	表示仔细听，并尝试理解听到的东西，强调听的动作和过程。是不及物动词，后面要加介词再接名词，比如，listen to music（听音乐）
sit和seat都表示"坐"	
sit	多用作不及物动词，用作及物动词时，可与seat换用
seat	及物动词，常与反身代词连用，常用过去分词seated形式，比如，Please be seated (= sit down).（请就座。）
turn、become、go和come都表示"变成、成为"	
turn	指彻底改变，且常用于朝坏的方向改变
become	是最普通用词，作为连系动词，表示情况开始、发展和结束的变化
go	作为连系动词，通常与形容词连用，指进入某种状态，从而发生变化，多指不好的状态
come	侧重变化的经过或过程，多用于好的情况
rest和stop都表示"中止、停止、休息"	
rest	指统称的休息，比如，take a rest（休息一下）

续表

stop	是普通用词，指迅速或突然中止某行为、活动或状态，比如，The car stopped at the traffic lights.（汽车在交通信号灯前停了下来。）
bring、carry和take都表示"带、拿、取"	
bring	指从某处把人或物带到或拿到说话者所在的地点，强调方向
carry	指把物品从一个地方带到另一个地方，只强调方式
take	指从说话人或说话人心目中所在处把某人或某物带离开，带到离说话者有一定距离的地方，侧重方向
care和mind都表示"介意、注意"	
care	指对某事感到关切、操心或忧虑，后面常跟that/wh-或if/whether引导的从句
mind	强调全心全意去注意，通常用于否定句、疑问句或条件句中
arrive和reach都表示"到达"	
arrive	是不及物动词，较正式，其后不可接宾语，但可接here、there、home之类表地点的副词。接名词需加介词
reach	是及物动词，指到达某一空间、时间、目标或发展过程中的某一点，reach the final of the European Cup（进入欧洲杯决赛）
attend和join都表示"出席、加入"	
attend	主要用于表示参加会议、集会等，有时也指上学、听课、听报告等。如，attend the meeting（出席会议）
join	是普通用词，指加入党派、团体或游戏活动等，比如，join the army（参军）
start和begin都表示"开始"	
start	可指工作、活动等的开始，战争、火灾等的发生，比如，start a new job（着手一项新工作）
begin	是最常用词，其反义词是end，多用于行动、工作等的开始，比如，When does the concert begin?（音乐会什么时间开始？）
fix、mend和repair都表示"修理、修复"	
fix	指"修理"时，是非正式用语，仅用于指带有安装、固定性质的修理，使用范围较广
mend	通常指较简单的修复或补救过程，一般不需要专门技术或特殊工具，多用于修理结构简单的小东西，比如，mend the window（修理窗户）
repair	一般指需要较高的职业技能和使用较复杂的工具修理比较庞大或复杂的东西，比如，repair a machine（修理机器）

3. 形容词辨析主要是针对一些相似或相关的形容词进行比较和分析，以确定在特定语境中哪个形容词更合适、更准确。形容词辨析主要考查的是对形容词词义、用法以及搭配等方面的理解和掌握。关于常考的形容词辨析总结如下。

fresh和new都表示"新的"	
fresh	指"新鲜的"，比如，fresh bread（刚出炉的面包）
new	是普通用词，与old相对，比如，new dress（新裙子）
live、alive和living都表示"活着的、活的"	
live	通常作前置定语，指活生生的、生气勃勃的，一般用于动物，比如，a live fish（一条活鱼）
alive	指生命从奄奄一息到精力旺盛的各种状态，可用来作表语、后置定语或宾补，比如，We need him alive!（我们需要他活着！）
living	指包括人和动植物的生命没有消失的状态，可用来指人或物、作定语或表语，比如，the greatest living pianist（健在的最伟大的钢琴家）
black和dark都表示"完全地或不完全地缺少光亮"	
black	侧重颜色是黑色的，有时也指无光的黑暗，比如，a black night（漆黑的夜晚）
dark	是普通用词，指缺乏自然光线或人工照明，使某物漆黑无光或光线十分微弱，比如，a dark room（黑暗的房间）
ill和sick表示"有病的"时是同义词	
ill	只能作表语，比如，Lee was ill.（李生病了。）
sick	可作定语和表语，比如，a sick child（生病的孩子）
bad、ill和poor都表示"坏的"	
bad	含义广泛，指任何不好的或不合需要的品质，比如，bad habits（恶习）
ill	语气弱一些，常指道德或性质方面的不良，比如，ill health（健康状况不佳）
poor	是普通用词，侧重指事物的质量或数量低于标准或不合要求，比如，poor food（劣质食品）
alone和lonely都表示"孤单的"	
alone	是普通用词，指独自一人的状态，比如，He is alone in a big house.（他独自在一所大房子里。）
lonely	强调孤独感，侧重于由于没有别人或其他东西陪伴而感到孤单。比如，He is alone and often feels lonely.（他孑然一身，常感到寂寞。）
small和little都表示"小的"	
small	多指数量、面积、体积、价值、数字或意义等的小或少
little	指由于因年龄小而身形娇小，含有感情色彩
outside和outer都表示"外部的"	
outside	通常表示超出某一地域、范围或限度，其反义词是inside，比如，The outside walls are damp.（外墙潮湿。）

续表

outer	主要指物体的外围、外面，有离开中心的意思，比如，the outer suburbs of the city（城市的远郊）
bright、clever和wise都表示"聪明的"	
bright	是口语常用词，多用于小孩或年轻人
clever	强调能较快地理解并正确掌握和应用所学的知识或技能
wise	指某人的头脑灵活或做某事的正确性，意味着具有广博的知识和丰富的经验
beautiful和handsome都表示"美丽的、漂亮的"	
beautiful	普通用词，含义广泛，侧重从客观上表明接近理想状态的美，语气最强，修饰人时主要用于妇女和儿童
handsome	多用于描写男性的英俊潇洒

🎧 百变演练

Choose the correct answer to complete the sentence. 选择正确答案填空。

1. —I go swimming every day.

   —Wow! That's a good _____. It keeps you healthy.

   A. match   B. task   C. habit

2. —Do you have any _____ for tonight yet?

   —Not yet. What about having a picnic on the beach?

   A. problems   B. news   C. plans

3. —Your new bike is so cool.

   —Thank you! In fact, I have _____ it for two months.

   A. bought   B. buy   C. had

4. The girl in the classroom _____ be Sarah. She has gone to the library.

   A. may   B. must   C. can't

5. —Why don't you buy the sweater?

   —It's too _____, and I don't have enough money to buy it.

   A. nice   B. expensive   C. cheap

6. Seeing a bird resting by the window, the boy moved _____ to have a look at it.

   A. safely   B. quietly   C. easily

Day 4　掌握六大语法知识点

 考点重现

　　阅读考试中，语法是重要考点之一，包括冠词、代词、介词、连词、比较级、主谓一致等，现将曾考过的部分内容汇总如下。

考点	考查内容	真题举例
冠词	a、an、the用法	the new house went to a lovely beach a great idea a few
代词	人称代词、物主代词等	Are they friendly? I hope you are well. I really like it (new house). It rained... both of them Have you ever played baseball? Let's take a picnic with us when we go to the river tomorrow.
介词	时间介词、地点介词等	on my way on TV in the evening in the centre of the town at the weekend at the top Thank you for...
连词	并列连词：and、or、but 从属连词：when、after、before、if等	prefer cola or orange juice I'll bring my football if I can find it. I'll show you my photos when/after I get back. He'll build me a treehouse when/after/before my school holiday begins.
比较级	形容词比较级等，标志词than	bigger than much warmer than more than
主谓一致	be动词：am、is、are 助动词：do、does、did 情态动词：can、may等 （后用动词原形）	Is it very cold? We are having a great time It was/is really good fun! Do you have any news? What do you think? I'll be able to...

🎧 考点锦囊

1. 冠词用于限定名词，表示泛指或特指。常见的冠词有三种：定冠词the、不定冠词a或an以及零冠词（不加冠词）。在阅读中正确识别和使用冠词是解题的关键之一。关于常见的冠词考点总结如下。

考点	考查内容	举例
定冠词 the	表示特指，通常表示已知或特定的对象	the car指的是特定的汽车，而不是任意一辆汽车
	在乐器、国家等专有名词、独一无二的事物前，要加the	play the piano 弹钢琴 the United States 美国 the sun 太阳
	在形容词最高级前，要加the	the most beautiful 最漂亮的
不定冠词a/an	泛指，表示某个类别中的一个实例	a cat指的是任意一只猫，而不是特定的某只猫
	不定冠词可以与量词短语一起使用，表示数量的不确定	a few days 几天
零冠词	在某些情况下，名词前可以不用冠词，通常为固定搭配	by train 乘火车 in fact 事实上

2. 在阅读考试中，代词是一个常考的语法点。该考点涵盖了人称代词、物主代词和不定代词。关于常见的代词考点总结如下。

考点	考查内容	举例
人称代词	第一人称（I、we），第二人称（you）和第三人称（he、she、it、they）的正确使用	**Lily** is my best friend. **She** is a beautiful girl. I love spending time with **her**. 莉莉是我最好的朋友。她是一个漂亮的女孩。我喜欢和她在一起。 （指代的词是Lily，所以代词主格用she，宾格用her）
	一般来说，如果所指代的名词是单数，则使用代词单数形式，比如he、she、it等。如果所指代的名词是复数，则使用代词复数形式，比如we、they等	
	主格作句子的主语，放在动词前；宾格作句子的宾语，放在动词后。比如，I是主格，me是宾格	
物主代词	形容词性物主代词用于修饰名词，表示所属关系	This is **my** book. **Mine** is new. 这是我的书。我的书是新的。 （my是形容词性物主代词，后面接名词book；mine是名词性物主代词，mine=my book）
	名词性物主代词可以替代形容词性物主代词加名词	
不定代词	不定代词作为句子的主语时，谓语动词通常用单数	**Everyone** is here. 大家都来了。
	both指"两者都"，谓语动词用复数，用于肯定句中 all指"三者及以上"，谓语动词用复数	**Both** of us are doctors. 我们俩都是医生。 **All** of them are hard workers. 他们全都工作努力。

3. 在阅读考试中，介词主要涉及三个方面：表示时间的介词、表示地点的介词和常用的介词短语。关于常见的介词考点总结如下。

考点		考查内容	举例
时间介词	at	用于具体的时间点	at 7 o'clock 在7点
	in	用于表示某个较长的时间段	in the morning 在早上 in 2024 在2024年
	on	用于具体的一天或某一天的早上、下午、晚上	on Monday 在星期一 on Monday morning 在周一上午
	before	表示在某个时间之前	before noon 在中午之前
	after	表示在某个时间之后	after dinner 在晚餐后
地点介词	in	用于较大的空间或地点	in the room 在房间里
	on	用于与表面接触或有平面接触的地点	on the table 在桌子上
	at	表示具体的位置或目的地	at the bus stop 在公交车站
	by	表示某物位于某物的旁边或附近	by the river 在河边
	near	表示某物在某物的近处，但不一定与其接触	near the school 在学校附近
介词短语	hear from 收到……的来信 be good at 擅长…… for example 例如 by train 乘坐火车 at home 在家		pay for 支付……的钱 be afraid of 害怕…… such as 例如 by the way 顺便问一下 at night 在夜里

4. 连词用于连接句子中的各个部分，以表达它们之间的关系。并列连词、转折连词和因果连词是考试中重点考查的三种类型。关于常见的连词考点总结如下。

考点		考查内容	举例
并列连词	and	意为"和"，连接两个或多个单词、短语、句子	He likes apples **and** bananas. 他喜欢苹果和香蕉。
	both...and...	意为"……和……都"，连接两个并列单词或短语	**Both** the boys **and** the girls are wearing blue shirts. 男孩和女孩都穿着蓝色的衬衫。
	neither...nor...	意为"既不……也不……"，表示对两者的否定	**Neither** the boys **nor** the girls are wearing hats. 男孩和女孩都没有戴帽子。
转折连词	but	意为"但是"，两者之间为转折关系	I wanted to go out, **but** it was raining. 我想出去，但是下雨了。
因果连词	because	意为"因为"，后面的句子表示原因	He was late for work **because** the traffic was heavy. 他上班迟到了，因为交通很拥挤。
	so	意为"所以"，后面的句子表示结果	She was feeling ill, **so** she stayed home from work. 她感到不舒服，所以她待在家里没去上班。

5. 在阅读考试中，考生需要掌握比较级和最高级的用法。关于比较级和最高级相关考点总结如下。

考点	考查内容	举例
比较级	比较级通常用于两者之间的比较，常与than一起使用，表示"比……更……"	This pear is **bigger than** that one. 这个梨比那个大。
	"比较级+and+比较级"表示"越来越……"	**more and more** beautiful 越来越漂亮
	"the+比较级，the+比较级"表示"越……越……"	**The more**, **the better**. 多多益善。
最高级	最高级用于表示在多个事物中，哪个最符合某个特点或属性，常与of或in一起使用，表示"在某个范围内最……的"	She is **the cleverest** child in her class. 她是她们班上最聪明的孩子。

6. 在阅读考试中，主谓一致是一个重要的语法考点，主要考查主语和谓语在数和人称等方面的一致性。关于主谓一致相关考点总结如下。

序号	主语	谓语动词	举例
1	金钱、价格、时间、长度等复数名词、短语	单数	**Three days is** too long. 三天时间太长了。
2	family、team、group等集合名词	表示整体概念：单数 表示集体中的成员：复数	Our **family** all **like** playing football. 我们的家人都很喜欢踢足球。 There **were** many **people** at the meeting. 集会有很多人。
3	people、police等集合名词	复数	
4	"the+形容词"表一类人	复数	**The old feel** the cold more than **the young**. 老年人比年轻人怕冷。

序号	考查内容		举例
1	就近原则：谓语动词的数与最靠近它的主语保持一致	Either... or... + 谓语动词	Not only my father but also **my mother is** a doctor. 不仅我的父亲，我的母亲也是一名医生。 There **is a pen**, a knife and several books on the desk. 书桌上有一支钢笔、一把小刀和几本书。
2		Not only... but also... + 谓语动词	
3		Neither... nor... + 谓语动词	
4		There be... and...	

🎧 百变演练

Choose the correct answer to complete the sentence. 选择正确答案填空。

1. Jane joined an art club at _____ age of six and paints well.

    A. an   B. a   C. the

2. Work hard, _____ you'll learn English well.

   A. and   B. but   C. or

3. Mr. Zhang has worked as _____ English teacher for more than 10 years.

   A. an   B. a   C. /

4. Which shirt is more expensive, the white one _____ the green one?

   A. and   B. or   C. but

5. You have to turn left _____ the first crossing.

   A. on   B. in   C. at

6. _____ it was early, she turned off the radio and went to bed.

   A. Because   B. Though   C. As

7. I like autumn _____ I can have a lot of fruit.

   A. but   B. because   C. though

8. —Mum, _____ I play football this afternoon?

   —Sure, but you _____ finish your homework first.

   A. may; could   B. can; must   C. can; mustn't

Day 5   加强句型认知能力

 考点重现

在阅读考试中，考生需要能够识别出阅读材料中的不同句型，如陈述句、疑问句、祈使句等，理解它们在语境中的作用和意义，对于提高阅读成绩至关重要。

考点	真题举例
陈述句	Our garden **is** really big. **I'm starting** at a new school next week. I **don't** think it's hard to write a good blog.
疑问句	**Are** they friendly? **Do** you have any news? **Have** you ever played baseball? **What's** the weather like?

续表

考点	真题举例
祈使句	**Let's** take a picnic with us when we go to the river tomorrow. **Don't** forget your swimming things.
感叹句	**How** quiet the beaches always are.
There be句型	**There are** many excellent surf teachers around the town. However, **there is** a big difference between Wivenhoe and other hotels.

🎧 考点锦囊

1. 识别句型：考生需要能够识别出阅读材料中的不同句型，如简单句、复合句、并列句等，理解它们在语境中的作用和意义。

考点	考查内容	举例
简单句	◆ 只含有一套主谓结构 ◆ 句子各成分都只由单词或短语构成	Things change. 事物是变化的。
并列句	◆ 由并列连词把两个或两个以上的简单句连在一起	I like action movies, **but** I don't like thrillers. 我喜欢动作片，但我不喜欢恐怖片。
复合句	◆ 疑问词作引导词，主句是全句的主体，通常可以独立存在；从句是一个句子成分，不能独立存在，但也有主语部分和谓语部分 ◆ 有定语从句、状语从句、宾语从句等	I heard **that** Jack had gone abroad. 我听说杰克已经出国了。

2. 理解句子结构：考生需要理解句子内部的语法结构和逻辑关系，包括主语、谓语、宾语、定语、状语等成分。

考点	考查内容	举例
主语	句子的主体，表示动作的执行者或状态的存在者	The cat（主语）sat（谓语）on the mat. 猫坐在垫子上。
谓语	主语执行的动作或存在的状态	
宾语	动作的承受者或状态的存在者	I（主语）love（谓语）music（宾语）. 我喜欢音乐。
定语	用于修饰名词，描述其属性或特征	The cute（定语）cat sat happily（状语）on the mat. 可爱的猫愉快地坐在垫子上。
状语	描述动词、形容词或副词的状态或动作，用于补充说明动作发生的时间、地点、方式等	

3. 分析句子功能：考生需要理解不同句型的功能，如陈述句、疑问句、祈使句、感叹句等，理解它们在表达情感、信息等方面的作用。

考点	考查内容	举例
陈述句	◆ 陈述事实或者看法 ◆ 有肯定句和否定句 ◆ 否定形式：be动词/情态动词/ do (does, did) +not	I like pizza. 我喜欢比萨。 She **doesn't** like fruit. 她不喜欢水果。
疑问句	◆ 提出问题或询问信息 ◆ 一般疑问句：用yes或no回答 特殊疑问句：特殊疑问引导词引导	**Where** does she come from? 她来自哪里?
祈使句	◆ 表示请求、命令、叮嘱或者劝告等语气 ◆ 主语通常省略，以动词原形开头，没有时态的变化，不能与情态动词连用	**Let** me try. 让我试试。 **Don't** eat in the classroom. 不要在教室里吃东西。
感叹句	◆ 表达喜、怒、哀、乐等强烈情感 ◆ what感叹句：what修饰名词 ◆ how感叹句：how修饰形容词或者副词	**What** a clever girl she is! 她是个多么聪明的姑娘呀! **How** clever you are! 你真聪明!

4. 理解复杂句型：考生需要能够理解和分析复杂的句型，如倒装句（There be句型）、长句（复合句）等，理解它们的含义和逻辑关系。

考点	考查内容	举例
There be 句型	◆ 意为"有"，表示"某地有某物"。强调某个地方有什么东西。 ◆ There is+可数名词单数/不可数名词+地点状语 There are+可数名词复数+地点状语	**There is** no ice in the cup. 杯子里没有冰。 **There are** some peaches in the plate. 盘子里有些桃子。

考点	考查内容	
长句分析	◆ **第一步**，分析句子主干	主语就是动作的发出者；谓语就是动作本身，找到主谓之后，就知道宾语在哪里了
	◆ **第二步**，分析从句或修饰成分	不管是多长的句子，一定是"主谓宾+其他"的结构，分析从句时要明确哪个是修饰名词的（定语从句），哪个是修饰动作的（状语从句）等
	【真题举例】They met while he was working at a theatre where she was dancing and got married soon after. 他们是在他在剧院工作时认识的，当时她正在那里跳舞，不久他们就结婚了。 首先，分析句子的主干： 主句是：They met and got married soon after. 他们相识不久就结婚了。 然后，分析从句或修饰成分 ① while he was working at a theatre是时间状语从句，表示"他们是在他在剧院工作时认识的" ② where she was dancing是定语从句，修饰先行词theatre，表示"她正在那里跳舞的剧院"。	

🎧 百变演练

Choose the correct answer to complete the sentence. 选择正确答案填空。

1. —_____ silent, please! You are in the library.

   —I'm sorry, madam.

   A. Keep   B. To keep   C. Keeping

2. —Neither Lily nor her parents _____ outdoors when the rainstorm came.

   —_____ lucky they were!

   A. were; What   B. was; How   C. were; How

3. Many people enjoy _____ zongzi by themselves on the Dragon Boat Festival.

   A. making   B. made   C. to make

4. —There _____ a basketball game against Class Two this Sunday.

   — I see. I will come and cheer you on.

   A. will have   B. is going to be   C. is going to have

5. Why not _____ your best _____ people in need?

   A. to try; to help   B. try; help   C. try; to help

6. _____ amazing the story is! I want to read it again.

   A. How   B. What   C. What an

Weekend 二 每周一练

I. Circle the correct word to complete each sentence. 圈出正确的单词补全句子。

1. Fire is very dangerous. You can't be **too /so** careful with it!

2. —I feel very **full / hungry**. May I have a cake?

   —Sure, you may take one from the fridge.

3. My little sister is a **curious / creative** girl and she always asks me different kinds of strange questions.

4. Robert is so **busy / smart** that he even has no time to stay with his children at weekends.

5. Sleeping is a good thing, but some people sleep **easily / badly**.

6. My sister is **shy / outgoing**. She likes making friends.

II. Choose the correct answer to complete the sentence. 选择正确答案填空。

1. —Have you got Kathy's _____ for her concert?

—Yes. I'd like to go and enjoy it.

A. invention   B. instruction   C. invitation

2. Which is the _____ to the bus stop, please?

A. road   B. way   C. street

3. —Dad, have you told Mum that I will come back next Wednesday?

—No. Let's keep it _____ and give her a surprise.

A. chance   B. choice   C. secret

4. —Could you give me a few _____ on how to spend the coming summer holiday?

—OK. Let me see.

A. hobbies   B. knowledge   C. suggestions

5. —Shall we go on Friday or Saturday?

—Either day is OK. It makes no _____ to me.

A. choice   B. change   C. difference

6. Daniel has tried to lose _____ by eating less recently, but two kilos has been put on instead.

A. weight   B. weights   C. height

7. He didn't use to be active in school, but now he gets lots of _____.

A. problem   B. money   C. attention

8. —Linda often answers the teachers' _____ in class, doesn't she?

—Yes. She is very active.

A. problems   B. notices   C. questions

III. Complete the sentences with the correct articles. 用正确的冠词补全句子。（提示词：a/ an/ the，或"不填"）

1. My elder brother is _____ engineer. He works very hard.

2. I usually go to _____ school on weekdays, and sometimes go to _____ cinema at weekends.

3. A horse is _____ useful animal.

4. Mrs. Smith has _____ daughter and a son.

5. Jane joined an art club at _____ age of six and paints well.

6. Beijing, _____ capital of China, has _____ long history.

IV. Complete the sentences with the correct prepositions. 用正确的介词补全句子。（提示词：in/ to/ on/ from/ behind/ between）

1. The hotel is next _____ the supermarket.

2. Is there a park _____ the neighbourhood?

3. There is a restaurant _____ the library and the school.

4. The school is across _____ the bank.

5. The broom is _____ the door. We can't see it.

6. They will arrive _____ London next Monday.

7. Helen's mother always goes shopping _____ Friday afternoons.

8. —How are you going to the train station to meet your aunt?

   —I'm going there _____ my car.

V. Complete the sentences with the words in the box. 用框中的单词补全句子。

look after	find out	pick	waste	put away

1. It is harmful to our environment if we pour _____ water into the rivers.

2. It's a good habit to _____ all your things in correct places.

3. Mrs. Brown isn't here. She has to _____ her baby at home.

4. The ticket is on the floor. Would you please _____ it up for me?

5. The window is broken. Try to _____ who broke it.

第3周目标					
考试模块	时间	主题	内容	
Part 1 短信息选择题	Day 1	短邮件	Ask for Information		☐
	Day 2	标识	Now on first floor		☐
	Day 3	通知	Trip Notice		☐
	Day 4	短信	Activity Invitation		☐
	Day 5	广告	Special offer		☐
	Weekend	每周一练	模拟训练		☐

Day 1　短邮件

 考场模拟

For each question, choose the correct answer.

A Greta has forgotten when the next maths class is.

B Greta hopes Fiona will help her find her maths notes.

C Greta wants to know what the maths homework is.

 思路点拨

Step 1:【审图片，划重点】

　　Help! Did you write down what we have to do before Thursday's maths class?

　　I've lost my notes!

- 关键信息：what we have to do before maths class（数学课之前要做什么）。

- 文本分析：Greta问Fiona是否记下周四数学课之前要做的事情。

- 核心句拆解：what we have to do... maths class是what引导的宾语从句，作write down（写下，记下）的宾语。

Step 2:【审选项，找匹配】

1. 关键信息

   A：Greta has forgotten when the next maths class is.

   B：Greta hopes Fiona will help her find her maths notes.

   C：Greta wants to know what the maths homework is.

2. 选项解析

   A：Greta忘记下节数学课的时间。

   B：Greta希望Fiona能帮她找到数学笔记。

   C：Greta想知道数学作业是什么。

3. 考点：Greta给Fiona发了一条信息，目的是什么？

4. 回到图片信息，找匹配

   Greta想知道下节数学课前要做的事情，即作业（本题中homework=what to do before maths class）。她把作业内容记在note（笔记）上了，但是笔记丢了。所以Fiona只需要告诉Greta作业是什么就行，不需要帮她再找到笔记。

   故正确答案是C。

🎧 考点锦囊

关于"学校"主题常考的单词或短语总结如下。

study 学习	group 组	mistake 错误
research 调查；研究	help 帮助	spell 拼写
let 让，允许	matter 物质；有关系	correct 正确的
maths 数学	write down 写下，记下	remember 记得
meaning 意义；含义	know 知道；了解	note 笔记；便条
ask 询问；要求	question 问题	revise 复习
homework 家庭作业	review 复习；检查	make notes 做笔记
help sb. do sth. 帮助某人做某事		hand in homework 交作业

百变演练

Choose the correct answer to complete the sentence. 选择正确答案填空。

1. The teacher asked the students to _____ their homework in their notebooks.

   A. write down   B. write to   C. write off

2. I _____ go to the doctor's tomorrow.

   A. have to   B. have got to   C. have a good time

3. — I _____ my homework at school.

   — Don't worry. You can do it tomorrow.

   A. forget   B. will forget   C. forgot

4. My sister enjoys singing and _____ favourite subject is music.

   A. his   B. her   C. you

5. It's a good idea to visit Beijing _____ October.

   A. at   B. on   C. in

Day 2   标识

 考场模拟

For each question, choose the correct answer.

Now on first floor:
Women's sports clothes
Toys for 0-12 year olds
Half-price books

Go upstairs if you want to

A buy a dress for a party.

B pay less for something to read.

C find a game for a teenager.

思路点拨

Step 1:【审图片，划重点】

Now on first floor:

Women's sports clothes

Toys for 0-12 year olds

Half-price books

- 常识信息：在美式英语中，"一楼"="first floor"，即楼房地面与街道相平的楼层为一楼，"一楼"就是"first floor"，"二楼"就是"second floor"。但在英式英语中，"一楼"是"ground floor"，而ground floor上面的一层（我们的二楼）才是"first floor"。

	英式表达	美式表达
一楼	ground floor	first floor
二楼	**first floor**	second floor
三楼	second floor	third floor
四楼	third floor	fourth floor

- 关键信息：二楼卖的是 Women's sports clothes（女式运动衫）

  Toys for 0-12 year olds（0～12岁的孩子玩具）

  Half-price books（半价图书）

- 文本分析：上楼能买到什么？

Step 2:【审选项，找匹配】

1. 关键信息

   A：buy a dress for a party.

   B：pay less for something to read.

   C：find a game for a teenager.

2. 选项解析

   A：买一件派对穿的裙子。

   B：花更少的钱买读物。

   C：找一个青少年玩的游戏。

3. 考点　楼上能买到什么？

4. 回到图片信息，找匹配

   楼上（二楼）卖的是女式运动衫、0～12岁的孩子玩具、半价图书。A选项"买派对穿的裙子", 不符合; C选项teenager指13~19岁的青少年, 不符合0~12岁。B选项"花更少的钱买读物", 符合。故正确答案是B。

🎧 考点锦囊

关于"购物"主题常考的单词或短语总结如下。

购物	
shopping centre 购物中心	try on 试穿
shopping mall 购物中心	warm jacket 保暖夹克
department store 百货商店	a pair of boots 一双靴子
supermarket 超市	a pair of pants 一条裤子
convenience store 便利店	a pair of socks 一双袜子
online shopping 网上购物	a pair of sunglasses 一副太阳镜
clothing floor 服装层	home goods floor 家居用品层
menswear section 男装区	electronics floor 电子产品层
womenswear section 女装区	food court 美食广场
accessories section 配饰区	underground parking 地下停车场

🎧 百变演练

Choose the correct answer to complete the sentence. 选择正确答案填空。

1. _____ you don't go to the party, you will miss a lot.

   A. If　　　　　　　　B. But　　　　　　　　C. After

2. There's always something _____ at the end of the week.

   A. to do it　　　　　B. to do　　　　　　　C. doing

3. *Alice in Wonderland* is a book _____ children.

   A. at　　　　　　　　B. to　　　　　　　　　C. for

4. —Which do you like _____, swimming or skating?

   —Swimming.

   A. well　　　　　　　B. better　　　　　　　C. best

5. —_____ do you tidy your own room?

—Twice a week.

A. How often　　　　　B. How long　　　　　C. How much

Day 3　通知

 考场模拟

For each question, choose the correct answer.

<table>
<tr><td>

Museum trip
Students who have not booked this trip should come to school as normal.

</td><td>

A Students not going on the trip cannot have a day off school.

B Students have to decide today if they would like to join the trip.

C Students going on the trip must come to school first.

</td></tr>
</table>

 思路点拨

Step 1:【审图片，划重点】

　　Students who have not booked this trip should **come to school as normal.**

- 关键信息：Students who have not booked come to school as normal（没有预订的同学照常到校上课）。
- 文本分析：博物馆旅行通知。
- 核心句拆解：who have not booked this trip是who引导的定语从句，修饰students。主句是students should come to school as normal。此处book作动词，意为"预约，预订"，as normal意为"像往常一样"。

Step 2:【审选项，找匹配】

　　1. 关键信息

　　　　A：Students not going on the trip cannot have a day off school.

B：Students <u>have to decide today</u> if they <u>would like to join the trip</u>.

C：Students <u>going on the trip</u> <u>must come to school first</u>.

2. 选项解析

A：不去旅行的学生不能放一天假。

B：学生们今天必须决定是否愿意参加这次旅行。

C：去旅行的学生必须先到学校。

3. 考点　博物馆旅行的通知内容是什么？

4. 回到图片信息，找匹配

博物馆旅行通知：没有参加这次旅行的学生必须像往常一样来学校。选项A与之相符。选项B、选项C均未提及。文本中come to school与选项A中的cannot have a day off school是一个意思。

考点锦囊

关于"博物馆旅行"主题常考的单词或短语总结如下。

博物馆	
science museum 科学博物馆	national museum 国家博物馆
art museum 艺术博物馆	public museum 公立博物馆
history museum 历史博物馆	technology museum 科技博物馆
natural history museum 自然历史博物馆	military museum 军事博物馆
space museum 太空博物馆	insect museum 昆虫博物馆

出门游玩	
mobile phone 手机	ticket 票
charger 充电器	book 预订
power bank 充电宝	schedule 日程安排
enough cash 足够的现金	sunglasses 太阳镜
some money 一些钱	sunscreen 防晒霜

百变演练

Choose the correct answer to complete the sentence. 选择正确答案填空。

1. I need to _____ a flight to Beijing for my business trip.

   A. book   B. borrow   C. sell

2. After the repair, the machine is working _____ normal.

   A. for   B. as   C. in

3. The man _____ on the street is my neighbour.

   A. walking   B. walk   C. walked

4. It was difficult to climb the mountain, _____ Sam got to the top at last.

   A. or   B. so   C. but

5. —Lucy, what are you doing?

   —I _____ a model ship.

   A. make   B. made   C. am making

Day 4   短信

考场模拟

For each question, choose the correct answer.

Hi Andy
I'm playing football with Tom this afternoon on the field behind Woodside School.
Do you want to come too? Let me know.
Jake

What should Andy do?

A invite some friends to play football

B tell Jake if he can join him later

C show Tom where Woodside School is

思路点拨

Step 1:【审图片，划重点】

I'm <u>playing football with Tom</u> this afternoon on the field behind Woodside School. **Do you want to come too? Let me know.**

- 关键信息：Do you want to come too? Let me know.（你也想来吗？告诉我一声。）
- 文本分析：Jake问Andy是否想一起踢足球。

Step 2:【审选项，找匹配】

1. 关键信息

   A：<u>invite some friends</u> to play football

   B：<u>tell Jake if he can join</u> him later

   C：<u>show Tom where</u> Woodside School is

2. 选项解析

   A：邀请一些朋友去踢足球

   B：告诉Jake晚点能不能和他一起去

   C：告诉Tom学校在哪里

3. 考点　Andy应该回复什么信息？

4. 回到图片信息，找匹配

   Jake想知道Andy今天下午能否和他们一起踢足球。所以Andy只需要回复信息告诉Jake晚点能不能和他一起去即可。

   故正确答案是B。

考点锦囊

关于"运动"主题常考的单词或短语总结如下。

运动场所	
playground 操场	court 球场
stadium 体育场	pool 游泳池
gym 健身房	track and field 田径
track 跑道	basketball court 篮球场
field 场地	soccer pitch 足球场

运动	
baseball 棒球	run 跑步
basketball 篮球	marathon 马拉松赛跑
hockey 曲棍球	jogging 慢跑锻炼
ice-hockey 冰上曲棍球	jump 跳跃
football 足球	high jump 跳高
table tennis 乒乓球	long jump 跳远
badminton 羽毛球	skating 滑冰
volleyball 排球	ski 滑雪

🎧 百变演练

Choose the correct answer to complete the sentence. 选择正确答案填空。

1. I enjoy playing _____ basketball with my friends after school.

   A. the   B. /   C. a

2. They have invited me _____ to Paris with them.

   A. went   B. go   C. to go

3. I wonder _____ I should wear a coat or not.

   A. who   B. that   C. if

4. —Nana, happy birthday to you!

   —_____.

   A. Thank you   B. You're welcome   C. Goodbye

5. —Can you speak English, Lingling?

   —Yes. I _____.

   A. must   B. can   C. should

Day 5　广告

 考场模拟

For each question, choose the correct answer.

A The ice cream shop is open for only 2 hours.

B Two ice creams will cost the same as one.

C You can get free ice creams all afternoon.

 思路点拨

Step 1:【审图片，划重点】

DAN'S ICECREAMS

Buy <u>one</u>, get <u>one free</u>! (Special offer **12 - 2 p. m. only**)

- 常识信息：special offer常用于广告的促销商品中，意为"特别优惠"。
- 关键信息：Buy one, get one free!（买一送一！）

  Special offer 12 - 2 p. m. only（仅限下午12点至2点的特别优惠）。
- 文本分析：这是一则DAN家冰激凌店的广告。

Step 2:【审选项，找匹配】

1. 关键信息

   A：The ice cream shop is <u>open for only 2 hours</u>.

   B：<u>Two</u> ice creams will <u>cost</u> <u>the same as one</u>.

   C：You can <u>get free ice creams all afternoon</u>.

2. 选项解析

   A：冰激凌店只营业两小时。

   B：两个冰激凌价格和一个一样。

C：你整个下午都可以得到免费的冰激凌。

3. 考点　冰激凌店的优惠活动是什么？

4. 回到图片信息，找匹配

图片内容提到"Dan家冰激凌，买一送一。特价只在12点到下午2点。"A选项"冰激凌店只营业两小时"，未提到。C选项"整个下午都可以买到免费的冰激凌"，错误，特价截止时间是下午2点。B选项"两个冰激凌的价格和一个一样"，正确。故正确答案是B。

🎧 考点锦囊

关于"广告和打折"主题常考的单词或短语总结如下。

广告

advertisement 广告	target 目标
brand 品牌	customer 顾客
logo 标识	information 信息
activity 活动	promotion 促销
campaign 活动	special 特别的
magazine 杂志	newspaper 报纸

打折

sale 促销	discount price 折扣价格
discount 折扣	at a discount 打折
giveaway 赠品	10% off 九折
coupon 优惠券	15% discount 八五折
special offer 特别优惠	full price 全价
discount offer 打折优惠	member discount 会员折扣
flash sale 限时促销	clearance sale 清仓特卖

🎧 **百变演练**

Choose the correct answer to complete the sentence. 选择正确答案填空。

1. The museum is _____ on Sundays.

   A. late   B. special   C. open

2. The toy is the one _____ I saw in the shop last Sunday.

   A. same as that   B. the same like   C. the same as

3. Tickets _____ ten dollars each.

   A. pay   B. cost   C. spend

4. —Frank, is this your bag?

   —No, it's not _____.

   A. mine   B. yours   C. his

5. My mother is a _____ in Zhongshan Hospital. She has saved many people's lives.

   A. singer   B. doctor   C. writer

Weekend 三 每周一练

I. Circle the correct word to complete each sentence. 圈出正确的单词补全句子。

1. My sister is only six, but **she / they** can already help with some housework.

2. We have history class **in / at** three o'clock every Friday afternoon.

3. Mr. Smith has helped me a lot, **but / so** I'm thankful to him.

4. From my childhood, I **politely / clearly** remember my parents working hard day and night.

5. He is so honest a man that we all **teach / trust** him.

6. —What's thirty and ten?—It's **forty / fifty**.

7. Many thanks **for / of** your gift. I love it.

8. Hurry up, **or / and** you will miss the beginning of the concert.

II. Choose the correct answer to complete the sentence. 选择正确答案填空。

1. —I'm sorry, mom. I made a mistake in the exam.

   —_____. Be careful next time.

   A. You'd better not.　　　B. It's too terrible.　　　C. It doesn't matter.

2. —Mr. Li, can I go to play football with my classmates as soon as school is over?

   —_____We have to prepare for the coming Art Festival together.

   A. Why not?　　　B. I hope so.　　　C. I'm afraid not.

3. —The Great Wall runs about 21, 200 kilometres.

   —Wow! _____.

   A. It's OK　　　B. Good idea　　　C. That's amazing

4. —I was all wet when I went to the zoo yesterday.

   —_____.

   A. Sounds terrible.　　　B. I'm sorry to hear that.　　　C. You're so lucky.

5. —Congratulations! You won the first prize at the speech contest.

   —_____.

   A. Thank you very much.　　　B. You're welcome.　　　C. With pleasure.

6. —I'd like to thank you for your invitation to Heze Peony Garden.

   —_____.

   A. With pleasure　　　B. It's my pleasure　　　C. For pleasure

III. Complete the sentences with the words in the box. 用框中的单词补全句子。

silent	bottles	seasons	repeats	yourself	instead of

1. Among the four _____ of year, I like winter best.

2. Sam, did you really fix the computer by _____?

3. This city recycles nearly 85% of its used plastic _____.

4. I think you should ride your bike to work _____ going by car.

5. He spoke no English and was completely _____ during the visit.

6. My grandfather often _____ that he wants to go back and live in the countryside.

IV. Match the questions (1–6) to the answers (A–F). 匹配问题与答案。

(　　) 1. Cindy, don't run in the living room!

(　　) 2. Alice, is your brother heavy or thin?

(　　) 3. I think a true friend touches your heart.

(　　) 4. Nick, what's your model plane made of?

(　　) 5. My grandfather was hit by a bike yesterday.

(　　) 6. Is Mike very patient?

> A. Wood and glass.
>
> B. I agree with you.
>
> C. I'm sorry to hear that.
>
> D. Yes, he is very patient.
>
> E. Sorry, I won't do it again.
>
> F. Oh, he is of medium build.

V. Complete the sentences with the correct form of the words. 用所给单词的适当形式补全句子。

1. —Is that _____ (you) schoolbag?

   —No, it isn't.

2. They like pears, but they don't like _____ (strawberry).

3. The teacher asked Ben _____ (answer) a question in class.

4. He _____ (sit) down and began to read a newspaper.

5. The word "ginseng" comes from the _____ (China) word "ren-shen".

6. The telephone _____ (invent) by Alexander Graham Bell in 1876.

VI. Complete the sentences according to the Chinese meanings. 根据中文提示，完成句子。

1. 打篮球对于我来说太难了。

   It's difficult for me _____ _____ basketball.

2. "怎么啦?"他惊讶地问。

"What happened?" he asked _____ _____.

3. 这书桌太重我拖不动。

This desk is _____ heavy _____ I can't move it.

4. 这就是他今早迟到的原因。

That's _____ he was _____ this morning.

5. 我不介意他喜欢与否。

I _____ care if he _____ it or not.

信息匹配题

Day 1　人物介绍·考场模拟

 考场模拟

For each question, choose the correct answer.

		Tasha	Danni	Chrissie
7	Who writes both a magazine and a blog?	A	B	C
8	Who says that studying and writing a blog at the same time can be hard?	A	B	C
9	Who answers questions from other people who read her blog?	A	B	C
10	Who plans to stop writing her blog soon?	A	B	C
11	Who didn't have many people reading her blog in the beginning?	A	B	C

12 Who asks a member of her family to help her write
her blog?   A   B   C

13 Who says writing a blog is easier than some other
types of writing?   A   B   C

Young blog writers

Tasha

Last year I wrote for my college magazine, which I found really difficult, but I don't think it's hard to write a good blog. Mine is about things from daily life that make me laugh. My older brother also has a blog, but we're writing about different subjects. We don't discuss what we're planning, but we read each other's blogs sometimes. I like giving advice to people who write in asking for it – it's good to know I've helped.

Danni

I started writing my popular film blog because I love movies. I like it when readers send me articles by email about a film they've seen, and I put these on my blog for everyone to read. I'm still at college, so I'm careful about spending too long on my blog, which is difficult as writing well takes time. I don't think I'll write it for much longer. I'm busy, and it's time to do something new.

Chrissie

I began writing on a school magazine. I stopped after a few years, but I missed it, so I started my own – I'm still writing it now! The blog's new for me, and I write about daily life. I get ideas from friends or my sister when I can't decide what to write about – we always think of something interesting, sad or serious. At first, almost nobody visited my site, but now more do, I've had some lovely comments.

解析

Step 1:【审题目，划重点】

7. [题干] Who writes **both a magazine and a blog**? 谁既写杂志又写博客？

8. [题干] Who says that **studying** and **writing** a blog at the same time can be **hard**? 谁说同时学习和写博客很难？

9. [题干] Who **answers questions from other people who read her blog**? 谁会回答其他读过她博客的人的问题？

10. [题干] Who **plans to stop writing her blog soon**? 谁打算很快停止写博客？

11. [题干] Who **didn't have many people reading her blog** in the beginning? 谁一开始没有很多人读她的博客？

12. [题干] Who **asks a member of her family** to **help her write her blog**? 谁会请家人帮她写博客？

13. [题干] Who says **writing a blog** is **easier than** some **other types of writing**? 谁说写博客比其他类型的写作更容易？

Step 2:【找线索，选答案】

7. 注意题干中的关键词writes both a magazine and a blog, 三个人物介绍中只有Chrissie提到I began writing on a school magazine. （我开始在学校杂志上写作。）和The blog's new for me, and I write about daily life. （博客对我来说是新鲜事物，我写的是日常生活。）由此得知，Chrissie既写杂志又写博客，故本题选C。

8. 根据文章信息，Danni提到I'm still at college, so I'm careful about spending too long on my blog, which is difficult as writing well takes time. （我还在上大学，所以我很小心不要在博客上花太多时间，因为写好文章需要时间。）原文中的hard和题干中的difficult同义。Danni还是在校学生，写博客会花费很多时间，所以同时学习和写博客是很困难的。故本题选B。

9. 根据文章信息，Tasha提到 I like giving advice to people who write in asking for it – it's good to know I've helped. （我喜欢给写信寻求建议的人提供建议——很高兴知道我提供了帮助。），原文中的giving advice是题干中answers questions的同义转换，Tasha喜欢给在博客下面留言询问问题的人提出建议，也就是回答他们的问题，进而帮助他们，故本题选A。

10. 文章中Danni提到I don't think I'll write it for much longer. I'm busy, and it's time to do something new.（我想我不会写太久了。我很忙，是时候做点新事情了。）由此可知，Danni认为她不会写很久的，故选B。

11. Chrissie在介绍时提到，At first, almost nobody visited my site.（起初，几乎没有人访问我的网站。）原文中的at first和题干中的in the beginning同义，且句中almost nobody和题干中的didn't have many people是同义转换。开始，没有人访问Chrissie的页面，故选C。

12. 文章中Chrissie提到I get ideas from friends or my sister when I can't decide what to write about.（当我无法决定写什么的时候，我会从朋友或姐姐那里得到想法。）原文中的my sister和题干中a member of her family是所属关系，故选C。

13. 根据文章信息，关于其他类型的写作，文章中Tasha提到Last year I wrote for my college magazine, which I found really difficult, but I don't think it's hard to write a good blog.（去年，我为大学杂志写了一篇文章，我发现这很难，但我认为写一篇好博客并不难。）原文中的college magazine和题干中的other types of writing是所属关系，学校杂志是其他写作类型的一种，且原文中的hard是题干中easier的反义词，故选A。

【Answer key】

| 7. C | 8. B | 9. A | 10. B | 11. C | 12. C | 13. A |

Day 2　人物介绍·考点锦囊

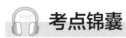 **考点锦囊**

1. 在关于"人物介绍"的文章中，常会提到学校、学习、工作等的介绍以及个人体验的相关内容，与其相关的单词或短语如下。

学校学习	
enter a school 入学	chemistry course 化学课
check in 登记；报到	sports lessons 体育课
in the same class 同班	music class 音乐课

学校学习

school uniform 校服	foreign language 外语
classroom activities 课堂活动	study tip 学习技巧
after school 放学后	make/take notes 做笔记
prepare for... 为……准备	keep a diary 写日记
middle school 中学	take an exam 参加考试

日常工作

full-time job 全职工作	make a living 谋生
working hours 工作时间	work for... 为……工作
permanent job 固定工作	go to work 去上班
part-time job 兼职工作	leave work 下班
job offer 工作机会	office building 办公大楼
manual labour 体力劳动	meeting room 会议室
out of work 失业	business trip 商务旅行
make money 挣钱	on business 因公，出差

2. 在人物描述的场景中，常会遇到题干的表述在原文中是另外一种说法，此时就需要考生将有关信息建立起对应关系，以下是同义转述的相关表达。

意思相近的词

job 工作	employment 工作
office 办公室	workplace 工作场所
business 企业	enterprise 公司
student 学生	pupil 小学生
class 课	lesson 课
personality 个性	character 性格
creative 创造性的	innovative 创新的
serious 需认真思考的	thoughtful 深思的
quiet 安静的	silent 不说话的
cheerful 高兴的	happy 高兴的

意思相反的词	
full-time job 全职	part-time job 兼职
quiet 安静的	loud 大声的
adventurous 勇于冒险的	cautious 谨慎的
patient 有耐心的	impatient 没有耐心的
shy 害羞的	outgoing 外向的
polite 有礼貌的	rude 粗鲁的
honest 诚实的	dishonest 不诚实的

百变演练

I. Complete the sentences with the correct form of the given words. 用所给单词正确
形式补全句子。

1. I bought two _____ (notebook) yesterday.

2. There _____ (be) a lot of rain outside last night.

3. Smile and greet others in a _____ (friend) way.

4. More and more young people enjoy _____ (read) poems.

5. I go to a chess club _____ (two) a week.

II. Complete the sentences according to the Chinese meanings. 根据中文提示，完成
句子。

1. 我叫托尼·史密斯，史密斯是我的姓。

   My name is Tony Smith and Smith is my _____ _____.

2. 去年，彼得在旅途中和许多人交了朋友。

   Peter _____ _____ with many people on his journey last year.

3. 这些书太有趣了，孩子无法停止阅读。

   These books are _____ interesting _____ the children can't stop reading them.

4. 你读过《哈利·波特》吗？

   _____ you _____ Harry Potter yet?

5. 汤姆很擅长讲故事。

Tom is very good at _____ _____.

III. Read the article of Day 1 and write T or F. 阅读Day 1的文章，并判断正误。

( ) 1. Tasha finds it easy to write a good blog.

( ) 2. Both Tasha's and brother's blogs write about the same topic.

( ) 3. Danni writes blogs because she enjoys movies.

( ) 4. Danni will keep writing in the future.

( ) 5. Chrissie had a lot of fans in the beginning.

Day 3 度假旅行 · 考场模拟

 考场模拟

For each question, choose the correct answer.

		Jasmine	Oliver	Emily
7	Who loves the world below the surface of water?	A	B	C
8	Who encountered bad weather during the trip?	A	B	C
9	Who went to the country to stay away from the city?	A	B	C
10	Who saw different kinds of sea animals?	A	B	C
11	Who likes a challenging, difficult mountain to climb?	A	B	C
12	Who has gained a different understanding for nature after a challenging journey?	A	B	C
13	Who said ancient houses are a reminder to years gone by?	A	B	C

The Magic of Travel

Jasmine

I was tired of the city and chose a week in the English countryside for peace. As I drove along country roads, city gave way to green fields and charming villages. I walked the rolling hills of the Cotswolds and enjoyed in the beauty of nature. I visited the unusual village, where the old stone cottages and gardens reminded people of the past. My escape was more than city escape; it was a journey to a world where time stood still. I returned to the city happily and fell in love with rural life again.

Oliver

I was a passionate diver who has traveled to the Bahamas for diving adventures in the Caribbean Sea. As I dived into the clear waters, I was greeted by a dazzling display of coral reefs and colourful marine life. I met schools of tropical fish and sea turtles. I also discovered sunken ships, now home to a rich ecosystem of marine life. My dive was more than a journey into the underwater world; it was an exploration of hidden treasures and a celebration of life beneath the waves.

Emily

I am an adventure-seeker eager to challenge myself in the Himalayas. I hiked to Everest Base Camp in Nepal, passing through foothills and feeling the soaring peaks touch the clouds. I climbed high passes, feeling chilly winds and seeing snow-capped peaks glisten in the morning sun. My journey tested me physical strength and was a journey of self-discovery and growth. I returned with a sense of accomplishment and a deeper respect for nature.

解析

Step 1:【审题目，划重点】

7. [题干] Who loves the world **below the surface of water**? 谁喜爱水面下的世界？

8. [题干] Who encountered **bad weather** during the trip? 谁在旅途中遇到了坏天气？

9. [题干] Who **went to the country to stay away from the city?** 谁去乡下是为了远离城市？

10. [题干] Who saw **different kinds of sea animals**? 谁看到了不同种类的海洋动物？

11. [题干] Who likes **a challenging, difficult mountain to climb**? 谁喜欢攀爬有挑战、有难度的山峰？

12. [题干] Who has **gained a different understanding for nature** after a challenging journey? 谁在经历了一段充满挑战的旅程后，对自然有了不同的理解？

13. [题干] Who said **ancient houses are a reminder to years gone by**? 谁说古老的房子是对逝去岁月的回忆？

Step 2:【找线索，选答案】

7. 注意题干中的关键词below the surface of water，三个人物介绍中只有Oliver提到My dive was more than a journey into the underwater world.（我的潜水不仅仅是一次海底世界之旅。）句中的the underwater world和题干中的the world below the surface of water同义，由此得知，本题选B。

8. Emily在介绍时提到I climbed high passes, feeling chilly winds and seeing snow-capped peaks glisten in the morning sun.（我爬上了高山口，感受着凛冽的寒风，看到白雪覆盖的山峰在清晨的阳光下闪闪发光。）句中的chilly winds和snow-capped peaks和题干中的bad weather是所属关系，凛冽的寒风和白雪覆盖的山峰都是旅行中的坏天气，故选C。

9. Jasmine在介绍旅行的魔力时，提到I, tired of the city, chose a week in the English countryside for peace.（我厌倦了城市生活，决定到英国乡村去住一个星期，以求平静。）文中的countryside和题干中的country同义，tired of是题干中stay away from的同义转换，故本题选A。

10. 文章中Oliver在描述时，提到I met schools of tropical fish and sea turtles.（我遇到了成群的热带鱼和海龟。）文中的tropical fish and sea turtles和题干中的sea

animals是所属关系，热带鱼和海龟都属于海洋生物，故选B。

11. 根据题干中的关键词mountain可以定位到原文中Emily的描述：I am an adventure-seeker eager to challenge myself in the Himalayas.（我是一个渴望在喜马拉雅山挑战自我的冒险家。）其中提到的mountain指代的就是题干中的Himalayas，challenge myself是题干中的challenging的同义转换。由此可知，正确答案是C。

12. 文章中Emily提到在结尾处提到I returned with a sense of accomplishment and a deeper respect for nature.（我带着一种成就感和对自然更深的敬意返程了。）文中a deeper respect for nature是题干中a different understanding for nature的同义替换，故选C。

13. 根据文章信息，Jasmine在介绍自己的旅行时提到I visited the unusual village, where the old stone cottages and gardens remind people of the past.（我参观了这个不寻常的村庄，那里古老的石头小屋和花园使人们想起了过去。）文中的old stone cottages与题干中的ancient houses同义，remind people of the past和题干中的a reminder to years gone by意思相同，故本题选A。

【Answer key】

7. B	8. C	9. A	10. B	11. C	12. C	13. A

Day 4 度假旅行·考点锦囊

 考点锦囊

1. 在描述"度假旅行"的文章中，常会提到关于假期、计划、目的地等的介绍，与其相关的短语如下。

度假旅行	
summer vacation 暑假	make a plan 制订计划
winter vacation 寒假	places of interest 名胜古迹
go on a trip 去旅游	digital camera 数码相机

度假旅行	
have a trip 旅游	tour guide 导游
take a trip 去旅行	show sb. around 带某人参观
travel around the world 环游世界	go backpacking 去背包旅行
all over the world 全世界	carry-on luggage 随身携带的行李
foreign country 外国	on holiday 在度假
go abroad 出国	on vacation 在度假
have fun 玩得开心	

2. 在度假旅行的场景中，常会遇到题干的表述在原文中是另外一种说法，此时就需要考生将有关信息建立起对应关系，以下是同义转述的相关表达。

意思相近的词	
resort 旅游胜地	tourist attraction 旅游景点
holiday 假期	vacation 假期
beach 海滩	coast 海岸
sightseeing 游览	tour 旅游
cruise 乘船游览	boat trip 乘船旅行
airfare 飞机票价	flying 乘飞机
dive 潜水	swim 游泳

意思相反的词	
first class 头等舱	economy class 经济舱
leisurely 悠闲的	rushed 仓促的
package tour 跟团游	independent travel 自助游
solo travel 独自旅行	group travel 团体旅行
domestic travel 国内旅行	international travel 国际旅行
all-inclusive 包括全部费用的	self-catering 餐食自理的

🎧 百变演练

I. Complete the sentences with the correct form of the given words. 用所给单词正确形式补全句子。

1. _____ (make) sure you lock the door when you go out.

2. The teacher asked the students _____ (circle) the correct answer.

3. Excuse me, what problems are we really _____ (try) to solve?

4. After a night's rain, the mountains are much greener and the air is much _____ (fresh).

5. Tourists can see many western-style _____ (build) in Shanghai Disneyland.

II. Complete the sentences according to the Chinese meanings. 根据中文提示，完成句子。

1. 凯特计划参加学校科学日活动。

   Kate was planning to _____ _____ _____ the activities on the school Science Day.

2. 莉莉想知道她是否能为科学日做些事。

   Lily wondered _____ _____ _____ _____ something for the Science Day.

3. 中国是世界上最古老的国家之一。

   China is one of _____ _____ countries in the world.

4. 晚上我要么看电视要么听音乐。

   In the evening, I _____ watch TV _____ listen to music.

5. 一开始，他的小组制作瓶装火箭有困难。

   At first, his group _____ _____ _____ _____ the bottle rocket.

III. Read the article of Day 3 and write T or F. 阅读Day 3的文章，并判断正误。

(　) 1. Jasmine prefers the country to the city.

(　) 2. Jasmine felt sad when she returned to the city.

(　) 3. Oliver discovered a sunken ship underwater.

(　) 4. Emily only climbed halfway up the Himalayas.

(　) 5. Emily believes that the journey has taught her a lot.

Day 5　娱乐爱好·考场模拟

 考场模拟

For each question, choose the correct answer.

		Tom	Alice	Bob
7	Who learned to ride a bike as a kid?	A	B	C
8	Who took part in the bicycle race?	A	B	C
9	Who said riding on the wide road is free?	A	B	C
10	Who said it's important to stick to something?	A	B	C
11	Who thinks riding a bike can keep fit?	A	B	C
12	Who thinks riding is dangerous but fun?	A	B	C
13	Who received a bicycle as a gift?	A	B	C

The Joy of cycling

Tom

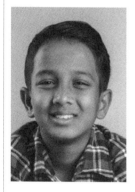

In my cycling journey, I faced many challenges, but the most significant was participating in a match. It was an intense experience with competitors who were faster and more experienced than me. I pushed myself to the limit, overcoming fear and fatigue. The race was tough, but when I was excited when crossing the finish line. This experience taught me not to give up easily and to achieve the aim despite difficulties. It remains a cherished memory in my life.

Alice

Once upon a time, I bought a shiny new bike, eager to explore my city on two wheels. Every Sunday, I ventured out on my trusty steed, cycling through parks, along riverbanks, and up challenging hills. I could enjoy the oncoming wind and the freedom of the open road. Cycling provided me with a sense of adventure and well-being. And thus, my cycling journey began.

Bob

I first learned to ride a bicycle as a young child, but it wasn't until I was fifteen that I truly fell in love with the excitement of cycling. After getting my first adult bike as a birthday present, I started exploring the city on two wheels, from quiet paths to hilly routes. It didn't matter if it was for a casual ride or a competitive race, the simple act of balancing and propelling myself forward always felt empowering. Cycling has become a crucial part of my life, providing me with a unique form of transportation and exercise.

解析

Step 1:【审题目，划重点】

7. [题干] Who learned to ride a bike as **a kid**? 谁小时候学会了骑自行车？

8. [题干] Who **took part in** the bicycle **race**? 谁参加了自行车比赛？

9. [题干] Who said riding **on the wide road** is **free**? 谁说在宽阔的路上骑行是自由的？

10. [题干] Who said it's important to **stick to something**? 谁说坚持是很重要的？

11. [题干] Who thinks riding a bike can **keep fit**? 谁认为骑自行车可以保持健康？

12. [题干] Who thinks riding is **dangerous but fun**? 谁认为骑行是危险的但很有趣？

13 [题干] Who **received** a bicycle **as a gift**? 谁收到了一辆自行车作为礼物？

Step 2:【找线索，选答案】

7. Bob在介绍时提到，I first learned to ride a bicycle as a young child.（我第一次学会骑自行车时还是个小孩子。）句中的 ride a bicycle、as a young child 分别对应题干中的 ride a bike、as a kid，故选C。

8. Tom在介绍自己的骑行爱好时，提到In my cycling journey, I faced many challenges, but the most significant was participating in a match.（在我的自行车之旅中，我遇到了很多挑战，但最重要的是参加比赛。）原文中的participating in 和题干中的took part in同义，match和题干中的race同义，故本题选A。

9. 注意题干中的关键词free，三个人物介绍中只有Alice提到I could enjoy the oncoming wind and the freedom of the open road.（我可以享受迎面而来的风和开阔道路上的自由。）句中的freedom和题干中的free同义，open和题干中的wide同义，由此得知，本题选B。

10. 根据文章信息，Tom在介绍"骑自行车"时提到This experience taught me not to give up easily and to achieve the aim despite difficulties.（这段经历教会了我不要轻易放弃，要克服困难实现目标。）文中的not to give up easily（不轻易放弃）和题干中提到的stick to（坚持）同义，故本题选A。

11. 根据题干中的关键词keep fit可以定位到原文中Bob的描述，最后一句提到Cycling has become a crucial part of my life, providing me with a unique form of transportation and exercise.（骑自行车已经成为我生活中至关重要的一部分，为我提供了一种独特的交通和锻炼方式。）其中提到的exercise是题干中的keep fit的同义替换，由此可知，正确答案是C。

12. 文章中Alice在描述时，提到Cycling provided me with a sense of adventure and well-being.（骑自行车给了我一种冒险和幸福的感觉。）由此推断出，Alice认为骑行是危险的但很有趣，故选B。

13. 文章中Bob提到After getting my first adult bike as a birthday present（在作为生日礼物得到我的第一辆成人自行车后），由此得知，Bob曾收到过一辆自行车作为礼物；文中的bike与题干中的bicycle同义，present与gift同义，故选C。

【Answer key】

7. C   8. A   9. B   10. A   11. C   12. B   13. C

Day 6 娱乐爱好·考点锦囊

 考点锦囊

1. 在描述"娱乐爱好"的文章中，常会提到关于娱乐活动、休闲爱好的相关内容，与其相关的单词或短语如下。

娱乐活动	
have a barbecue 烧烤	an amazing show 一场精彩的表演
join a club 加入一个社团	a bicycle ride 骑自行车兜风
take a photo / picture 拍照	climb a hill 爬山
take a selfie 自拍	fly a kite 放风筝
draw a picture 画画	ride a horse 骑马
pick fruits 采摘水果	plant trees 植树
pick flowers 摘花	surf the Internet 上网冲浪
line up 排队，列队	take /do exercise 做运动
be in line 排成一行	keep fit 保持健康
in a row 一排	keep healthy 保持健康
in the queue 排队	be great at (doing) sth. 擅长某事

其他活动场所及相关描述	
movie theatre 电影院	amusement park 游乐园
the opera house 歌剧院	theme park 主题公园
sports centre 体育中心	ticket office 售票处
football stadium 足球场	public library 公共图书馆
a badminton court 羽毛球场	nature park 自然公园
swimming pool 游泳池	nature reserve 自然保护区

2. 在各类娱乐爱好的场景中，常会遇到题干的表述在原文中是另外一种说法，此时就需要考生将有关信息建立起对应关系，以下是主题为"娱乐爱好"的同义转述的表达。

意思相近的词	
arrive 到达	reach 到达
enjoy 喜欢	like 喜欢
happy 开心的	glad 开心的
sad 伤心的	unhappy 难过的
beautiful 漂亮的	pretty 漂亮的
important 重要的	significant 重要的
real 真实的	actual 真实的
small 小的	tiny 小的
big 大的	large 大的
busy 忙碌的	occupied 忙碌的

意思相反的词	
hot 热的	cold 冷的
up 向上	down 向下
fast 快的	slow 慢的
left 左边的	right 右边的
big 大的	small 小的
happy 高兴的	sad 难过的
good 好的	bad 坏的
inside 内部	outside 外部
long 长的	short 短的

🎧 百变演练

I. Complete the sentences with the correct form of the given words. 用所给单词正确形式补全句子。

1. Safety _____ (come) first.

2. I'm sorry to take your schoolbag _____ (careless).

3. The worried mother is looking forward to _____ (hear) from her daughter.

4. Most people don't like _____ (rain) days because they make people feel sad.

5. Now many wild animals are in _____ (dangerous). We should protect them.

II. Complete the sentences according to the Chinese meanings. 根据中文提示，完成句子。

1. 学校科学日很精彩。凯特真高兴！

   The school Science Day was wonderful. _____ _____ Kate was!

2. 对学生们来说，知道学习的重要性是必要的。

   It's necessary for students _____ _____ the importance of studying.

3. 玛丽很粗心，经常错误地拿走别人的家庭作业。

   Mary is so careless that she often takes others' homework _____ _____.

4. 他过去特别安静。

   He _____ _____ be really quiet.

5. 如果乘公交车去机场的话，我会错过我的航班。

   If I _____ the bus to the airport, I'll _____ my flight.

III. Read the article of Day 5 and write T or F. 阅读Day 5的文章，并判断正误。

( ) 1. On Tom's bike trip, he didn't like to take part in races.

( ) 2. Alice's shiny new bike was a gift from her mother.

( ) 3. On Sundays, Alice goes to the park by bike.

( ) 4. Bob first learned to ride a bike when he was very young.

( ) 5. Cycling is an important part of Bob's life.

Weekend 二 每周一练

I. Complete the sentences with the words in the box. 用框中的单词补全句子。

protect	lucky	during	clean	greeted

1. Mr. Watson _____ all the guests warmly as they arrived yesterday morning.

2. It's raining outside. You need warm clothes to _____ you against the cold.

3. People _____ the house before Spring Festival every year.

4. Most people like to wear red on important days because red is a _____ colour.

5. Tom made lots of friends _____ his life as a student.

II. Complete the sentences according to the Chinese meanings. 根据中文提示，完成句子。

1. 约翰尽力在工作和娱乐中获得平衡。

   John does his best to keep the balance _____ work _____ play.

2. 我们应该遵守交通法规。

   We should always _____ the _____ signs and rules.

3. 我更喜欢自己创作音乐的歌手。

   I _____ _____ that write their own music.

4. 秋天，树叶变黄，从树上落下。

   In autumn, leaves turn yellow and _____ _____ the trees.

5. 我希望今年暑假我们能和朋友共度更多的时光。

   I hope we can _____ more time _____ friends this summer vacation.

III. For each question, choose the correct answer. 请选择每道问题的正确答案。

		Charlie	Miguel	Hannah
1	Who wishes to go back to childhood?	A	B	C
2	Who wants green fuels to be invented in the future?	A	B	C
3	Who hopes to have more time to enjoy life?	A	B	C
4	Who wants to talk to the great man of the past?	A	B	C
5	Who hopes to live in a beautiful and non-pollution environment?	A	B	C
6	Who thinks sleeping two hours a day is great?	A	B	C
7	Who wishes to travel through the past and the future?	A	B	C

FUTURE VIEW

Charlie

It will be great if there is some kind of fuel we can use in cars that won't produce any pollution. I guess there are scientists right now trying to do that, and I hope they'll succeed because the world would be a much cleaner place, wouldn't it? Imagine waking up to a world where the air was clean, the skies were blue, and the sounds of nature were pure and uninterrupted.

Miguel

I think it will be great if they invent something so that we only have to sleep for one or two hours every day. Then we'd all have much more time to do things and to enjoy ourselves. With less sleep, we would have more time to learn new skills, such as cooking, painting, or learning a new language. We could also spend more time with family and friends, engaging in activities like going on picnics, playing sports, or simply enjoying each other's company.

Hannah

If I could choose anything, I'd go for a time machine so that I could go back and do some things differently. I wish I could go back in time to when I was a kid and say some of the things in a different way! I would also use the time machine to meet my favourite historical figures. I would like to talk to people like Einstein or maybe even meet a dinosaur! I would learn from them and find out what life was like in their times.

Week 5

阅读理解题

Day 1 人物经历·考场模拟

 考场模拟

PART 3

QUESTIONS 14-18

For each question, choose the correct answer.

A family of dancers

The women in the Watson family are all crazy about ballet. These days, Alice Watson gives ballet lessons, but for many years, she has been a dancer with the National Ballet Company. Her mother, Hannah, also had a full-time job there, making costumes for the dancers.

Alice's daughter Demi started learning ballet as soon as she could walk. "I never taught her," says Alice, "because she never let me." Now aged sixteen, Demi is a member of

---

the ballet company where her mother has been the star dancer for many years.

Alice's husband, Jack, is an electrician. They met while he was working at a theatre where she was dancing and got married soon after. "When Demi started dancing, the house was too small for her and Alice to practise in, so I made the garage into a dance studio. Now the living room is nice and quiet when I'm watching television!" he says.

Last month, Demi was invited to dance in the ballet *Swan Lake*. Of course, Alice and Hannah were in the audience and even Jack was there, which made it very special for Demi. Jack says, "I'm not that interested in ballet myself but it's fantastic seeing Demi taking her first steps with Alice's old company!" Demi was wearing a dress that Hannah made for Alice many years before.

"It was very exciting for all of us," says Hannah. "Demi's way of dancing is very like Alice's. I know I'm her grandmother, but I think she has a great future!"

14 What is Alice Watson's job now?

    A dancer   B teacher   C dress-maker

15 Demi had her first ballet lessons

    A at a very young age.

    B at the National Ballet Company.

    C from her mother.

16 Jack helped his wife and daughter by

    A moving to a larger house.

    B letting them use the living room for dancing.

    C making a place for them to practise in.

17 What was the best thing about the *Swan Lake* show for Demi?

    A It was her first show with the company.

    B All her family were there.

    C She was wearing a new dress.

18 Hannah says that Demi

    A will be a star one day.

B is her favourite granddaughter.

C dances better than Alice did.

🎧 思路点拨

Step 1:【审题目，划重点】

14. [题干] What is **Alice Watson's job** now?　爱丽丝·沃森现在的工作是什么？

  [选项]A. dancer　舞者；B. teacher　老师；C. dress-maker　裁缝

15. [题干] Demi had her **first ballet lessons**　黛米第一次上芭蕾舞课

  [选项] A. at a very young age　在很小的时候；B. at the National Ballet Company　在国家芭蕾舞团；C. from her mother　是跟她妈妈学的

16. [题干] Jack **helped** his wife and daughter **by**　杰克帮助他的妻子和女儿

  [选项]A. moving to a larger house　搬到更大的房子；B. letting them use the living room for dancing　让她们在客厅跳舞；C. making a place for them to practise in　给她们一个练习的地方

17. [题干] What was **the best thing** about the *Swan Lake* show for Demi?　对黛米来说，《天鹅湖》演出最棒的是什么？

  [选项]A. It was her first show with the company.　这是她在公司的第一次演出。B. All her family were there.　她所有的家人都在那里。C. She was wearing a new dress.　她穿着一件新衣服。

18. [题干] **Hannah says** that Demi　汉娜说黛米

  [选项]A. will be a star one day.　总有一天会成为明星的。B. is her favourite granddaughter.　是她最喜欢的孙女。C. dances better than Alice did.　比爱丽丝跳得好。

Step 2:【回原文，找答案】

14. 文章第一段第二句话提到，These days, Alice Watson gives ballet lessons. （如今，爱丽丝·沃森在上芭蕾舞课。）其中these days就表示题干中的 now，原文中的give ballet lessons等同于teach ballet lessons，由此得知，Alice 现在的工作是一名老师，故选B。根据文章第一段的内容，Alice在过去是一个 dancer，而Alice的妈妈Hannah是一个dress-maker，故A和C都可排除。

15. 文章第二段第一句提到，Alice's daughter Demi started learning ballet as soon as she could walk.（爱丽丝的女儿黛米一会走路就开始学习芭蕾舞。）原文中 started learning ballet与题干中的had her first ballet lessons意思相同，原文中的 as soon as she could walk等同于A选项中的at a very young age。文中提到"16岁 的Demi是芭蕾舞团的一员"，并没有说她在国家芭蕾舞团学习的芭蕾舞，故 B可排除；第二段中Demi的妈妈Alice也表示自己从未教过Demi芭蕾舞，故C 可排除。本题正确答案为A。

16. 文章第三段第三句提到，When Demi started dancing, the house was too small for her and Alice to practise in, so I made the garage into a dance studio.（当黛米开始 跳舞时，房子太小了，她和爱丽丝无法在里面练习，所以我把车库变成了舞 蹈工作室。）由此可知，Demi的爸爸Jack把车库变成了她们练习的地方，故 本题选C。

17. 根据题干中的the *Swan Lake* show可定位到文章第四段。第二句提到，Of course, Alice and Hannah were in the audience and even Jack was there, which made it very special for Demi.（当然，爱丽丝和汉娜也在场，甚至杰克也在 场，这对黛米来说非常特别。）由此得知，对于Demi而言，她的家人都来看 她的演出，这是最棒的事情了。原文中的Alice、Hannah和Jack都是Demi的家 人，所以本题选B。

18. 根据文章最后一段，Hannah认为"Demi的舞蹈方式很像Alice的"，并没有说 Demi跳得比Alice好，故C可排除。文章也未提到"Hannah说Demi是她最喜欢 的孙女"，故B也可排除。最后一段第二句提到，I know I'm her grandmother, but I think she has a great future!（我知道我是她的祖母，但我认为她有美好的 未来！）原文中have a great future说明Hannah认为Demi某一天会成为一个明 星，故本题选A。

【 Answer key 】

14. B   15. A   16. C   17. B   18. A

Day 2 人物经历·考点锦囊

 考点锦囊

1. 有关"人物经历"的文章中，常会涉及一些关于职业、成长经历等话题，与其相关的单词或短语如下。

文艺相关	
singer 歌手	dancer 舞蹈家
ice dancer 冰舞选手	album 音乐专辑
actor 演员	actress 女演员
artist 艺术家	concert 音乐会
dance music 舞蹈音乐	guitar 吉他
show 演出	band 乐队
audience 观众；听众	popular 流行的
ballet 芭蕾舞	opera 歌剧

其他职业	
designer 设计师	novelist 小说家
astronaut 宇航员	pilot 飞行员
architect 建筑师	engineer 工程师
mechanic 机修工	journalist 记者
business 商业；生意	businessman 商人
businesswoman 女商人	farmer 农民
boss 老板	career 职业

2. 在描述自己的生活或职业经历时，常会用到一些表达情感态度的句型或句子。

✓ 正面情感态度

I'm pleased about... 我对……表示很高兴。

I love... 我喜欢……

I like best about... 我最喜欢……

✓ 负面情感态度

It's the worst. 这是最糟糕的。

It's horrible. 太糟糕了。

I'm angry about it. 我对此表示很气愤。

🎧 百变演练

I. Complete the sentences with the correct form of the given words. 用所给单词正确形式补全句子。

1. Last month, Demi _____ (invite) to dance in the ballet Swan Lake.

2. When Demi started _____ (dance), the house was too small for her and Alice to _____ (practise) in, so I made the garage into a dance studio.

3. It was very _____ (excite) for all of us.

4. Her mother, Hannah, also had a full-time job there, _____ (make) costumes for the dancers.

5. They met while he was working at a theatre where she was dancing and got _____ (marry) soon after.

II. Complete the sentences with the correct prepositions. 用正确的介词补全句子。

1. The women in the Watson family are all crazy _____ ballet.

2. These days, Alice Watson gives ballet lessons, but _____ many years, she was a dancer with the National Ballet Company.

3. I'm not that interested _____ ballet myself.

4. Demi's way _____ dancing is very like Alice's.

5. Demi was wearing a dress that Hannah made _____ Alice many years before.

III. Read the article of Day 1 and write T or F. 阅读Day 1的文章，并判断正误。

(　) 1. Alice Watson was a dancer with the National Ballet Company before she became a ballet teacher.

(　) 2. Demi started learning ballet from her mother, Alice.

(　) 3. Hannah, Alice's mother, used to be a dancer with the National Ballet Company.

(　) 4. Demi's father, Jack, is a professional ballet dancer.

( ) 5. Hannah, Alice's mother, made a dress for Demi's performance in Swan Lake.

Day 3　假期旅行 · 考场模拟

 考场模拟

QUESTIONS 14-18

For each question, choose the correct answer.

Jimmy's visit to a chocolate museum

This summer holiday, my family and I visited a museum about chocolate called MUCHO Museo de Chocolate in Mexico City. When we first arrived at the museum, we were greeted by our tour guide, the only person who spoke English at the place. She told us chocolate is made of cacao beans. Then she let us taste real cacao beans. They were different from normal chocolate, because they were not sweet.

The museum was divided into different rooms. In the first one, we learned that the Mayans saw cacao as a magical thing that fed the mind, body, and spirit. They would ground the beans into powder and mix it with ingredients to create a bitter drink. It was then poured from different heights to create foam. This played a big role in their culture.

Then we got to learn about the beginnings of chocolate, see dried cacao tree leaves, and smell the other ingredients carefully. I also took photos in front of the wall covered with more than 2,000 pieces of chocolate! One of my favourite rooms showed many different pots, cups, and kettles from all over the world. They were used to hold chocolate or chocolate powder.

The visit to the chocolate museum was short, but I sure did learn a lot about a very popular treat. I was very surprised at how cultures from ancient times could influence our modern lives in such a way and how communications between different cultures

---

could influence each other. I highly recommend it as a stop for any visitor who loves chocolate and even those who don't.

14 What did the tour guide explain about chocolate?

A It is as sweet as cacao beans.

B It tastes the same as cacao beans.

C It is made of cacao beans.

15 The Mayans used cacao beans for

A making a drink.   B cooking meals.   C selling.

16 What was displayed in one of Jimmy's favourite rooms?

A More than 2,000 pieces of chocolate.

B Dried cacao tree leaves.

C Pots, cups, and kettles from all over the world.

17 How did Jimmy feel about the visit to the museum?

A It was very boring.

B It was short but meaningful.

C It was not worth the time and money.

18 Jimmy was surprised at

A how modern cultures are influenced by ancient cultures.

B how chocolate is made from cacao beans.

C how many different types of chocolate were on display.

🎧 思路点拨

Step 1:【审题目，划重点】

14. [题干] What did the tour guide **explain about chocolate**?　关于巧克力，导游做了什么解释?

[选项]A. It is as sweet as cacao beans.　它和可可豆一样甜。B. It tastes the same as cacao beans.　它的味道和可可豆一样。C. It is made of cacao beans.　它是由可可豆制成的。

15. [题干] The Mayans **used cacao beans for**　玛雅人用可可豆

[选项]A. making a drink. 做饮料。B. cooking meals. 做饭。C. selling. 售卖。

16. [题干] What was **displayed** in one of Jimmy's **favourite rooms**? 吉米最喜欢的房间之一里陈列着什么?

[选项]A. More than 2,000 pieces of chocolate. 2000多块巧克力。B. Dried cacao tree leaves. 可可树的干树叶。C. Pots, cups, and kettles from all over the world. 来自世界各地的罐、杯和水壶。

17. [题干] How did Jimmy **feel** about the visit to the museum? 吉米对参观博物馆有何感受?

[选项]A. It was very boring. 非常无聊。B. It was short but meaningful. 虽然时间很短,但很有意义。C. It was not worth the time and money. 不值得花费时间和金钱。

18. [题干] Jimmy **was surprised at** 吉米对_____感到惊讶。

[选项]A. how modern cultures are influenced by ancient cultures. 现代文化如何受到古代文化的影响。B. how chocolate is made from cacao beans. 巧克力是如何从可可豆中制成的。C. how many different types of chocolate were on display. 展览中有多少种不同类型的巧克力。

Step 2:【回原文,找答案】

14. 文章第一段提到,She told us chocolate is made of cacao beans. (导游告诉我们巧克力是由可可豆制成的。) 故C为正确答案。导游让作者及其家人们品尝了可可豆,They were different from normal chocolate, because they were not sweet. (可可豆与普通巧克力不同,因为它们不甜。) 由此得知,A和B的描述都不正确。

15. 文章第二段提到,They would ground the beans into powder and mix it with ingredients to create a bitter drink. (他们会将豆磨成粉末,并将其与配料混合,制成一种苦味饮料。) 故本题选A。

16. 文章第三段提到,One of my favourite rooms showed many different pots, cups, and kettles from all over the world. (我最喜欢的一个房间展示了许多来自世界各地的不同的罐、杯和水壶。) 故本题选C。

17. 文章最后一段第一句提到,The visit to the chocolate museum was short, but I sure did learn a lot about a very popular treat. (参观巧克力博物馆的时间很短,

但我确实学到了很多关于这种非常受欢迎的食物的知识。）由此得知，Jimmy 认为这次参观短暂但却很有收获、很有意义，故本题选B。

18. 文章最后一段第二句提到，I was very surprised at how cultures from ancient times could influence our modern lives in such a way and how communications between different cultures could influence each other.（我非常惊讶于古代文化如何以这种方式影响我们的现代生活，以及不同文化之间的交流如何相互影响。）故本题选A。

【Answer key】

14. C   15. A   16. C   17. B   18. A

Day 4　假期旅行·考点锦囊

 考点锦囊

　　在描述"假期旅行经历"的文章中，常会提到关于景点、城市、建筑等的介绍以及个人体验的相关内容，与其相关的单词或短语如下。

地点位置	
country 国家	path 小路
highway 公路	walk along 沿着……走
countryside 乡村	across 在对面
sign 指示牌	island 小岛
canal 运河	castle 城堡
direction 方向	farmland 农田
campsite 营地	local 当地的
modern 现代的	palace 宫殿

旅游观光	
outdoors 在户外	tourist 游客
tour guide 导游	from around the world 来自世界各地

旅游观光	
information 信息	beach 海滩
website 网站	experience 经历
arrival 到达	explorer 探险者
guidebook 指南	harbour 港口
coast 海岸	jungle 丛林
waterfall 瀑布	sightseeing 观光
tourist information centre 旅游信息中心	journey 旅程

百变演练

I. Complete the sentences with the correct form of the given words. 用所给单词正确形式补全句子。

1. When we first arrived at the museum, we _____ (greet) by our tour guide.

2. Then she let us _____ (taste) real cacao beans.

3. I _____ (high) recommend it as a stop for any visitor who loves chocolate and even those who don't.

4. In the first one, we learned that the Mayans _____ (see) cacao as a magical thing that fed the mind, body, and spirit.

5. I also took _____ (photo) in front of the wall covered with many pieces of chocolate.

II. Complete the sentences with the correct prepositions. 用正确的介词补全句子。

1. She told us chocolate is made _____ cacao beans.

2. They were different _____ normal chocolate.

3. The museum was divided _____ different rooms.

4. They would ground the beans into powder and mix it _____ ingredients to create a bitter drink.

5. I also took photos in front of the wall covered _____ more than 2,000 pieces of chocolate!

III. Read the article of Day 3 and write T or F. 阅读Day 3的文章，并判断正误。

( ) 1. The tour guide at the chocolate museum was the only person who could speak English.

(   ) 2. Cacao beans used to make chocolate are sweet.

(   ) 3. The Mayans used cacao beans to create a bitter drink.

(   ) 4. The museum had a room displaying different kinds of pottery used to hold chocolate or chocolate powder.

(   ) 5. The author recommends the museum for chocolate lovers only.

Day 5　休闲爱好·考场模拟

 考场模拟

PART 3

QUESTIONS 14-18

For each question, choose the correct answer.

Gardening Lover

Kendall spends a lot of time playing in the earth. She has a huge garden that produces over 100 pounds of food each year! But for this seven-year-old girl, gardening isn't just about fruits and vegetables. It's about people. "My favourite thing about growing food is doing it with my family and friends." she says.

Kendall began gardening at the age of three, when her grandmother gave her some potatoes, Grandma told her, "Don't throw away the small ones, because if you put them in the ground, they will grow back." Kendall tried it and was amazed when the small potatoes grew new leaves.

Soon after, her parents put in a small yard garden. When friends came over, Kendall enjoyed sharing what she knew. And she says, "My friends help me water and care for the plants."

At the age of six, she became the youngest licensed farmer in Georgia. Today, her garden has grown to include sixty plant beds and twelve trees! When the vegetables

---

and fruits are ripe, Kendall says, "I pick them, then I do a food sale so other kids and families can have some." People who don't have enough food are invited to take what they need.

Kendall is a role model for other children. She speaks at libraries and schools and hosts a community garden club for kids. "I also invite kids to visit my garden and help me with it, to see how fun it is," she says. "Growing food takes a lot of work, but together you can do it."

14 Kendall spends much time in the garden to

    A enjoy growing food with her family and friends.

    B sell food and make money.

    C play games with her family there.

15 What did Kendall's grandmother tell her about the small potatoes?

    A To throw them away.

    B To plant them in the ground.

    C To water them in the garden.

16 What did Kendall's friends do when they came to her garden?

    A They helped take care of the plants.

    B They brought the food that they grew.

    C They built a yard for Kendall.

17 Kendall became the youngest licensed farmer in Georgia

    A after hosting a community garden club for kids.

    B when she was six years old.

    C at the age of twelve.

18 What does Kendall say in the end?

    A We should spend more time growing food.

    B It's useful to speak at the libraries and schools.

    C It's worth gardening together though it's hard work.

🎧 **思路点拨**

Step 1: 【审题目，划重点】

14. [题干] Kendall **spends much time in the garden** to   肯德尔花了很多时间在花园里是为了

    [选项]A. enjoy growing food with her family and friends.   喜欢和家人朋友一起种植食物。B. sell food and make money.   卖食物赚钱。C. play games with her family there.   和她的家人在那里玩游戏。

15. [题干] What did Kendall's grandmother tell her **about the small potatoes**?   关于这些小土豆，肯德尔的祖母跟她说了什么？

    [选项]A. To throw them away.   把它们扔掉。B. To plant them in the ground.   把它们种在地里。C. To water them in the garden.   在花园里给它们浇水。

16. [题干] What did **Kendall's friends do** when they came to her garden?   肯德尔的朋友们来到她的花园时都做了什么？

    [选项]A. They helped take care of the plants.   他们帮忙照料植物。B. They brought the food that they grew.   他们带来了他们种植的食物。C. They built a yard for Kendall.   他们为肯德尔建了一个院子。

17. [题干] Kendall **became the youngest licensed farmer** in Georgia   肯德尔成为佐治亚州最年轻的持证农民

    [选项]A. after hosting a community garden club for kids.   在为孩子们举办了一个社区花园俱乐部之后。B. when she was six years old.   在她六岁的时候。C. at the age of twelve.   在十二岁的时候。

18. [题干] What does **Kendall say** in the end?   肯德尔最后说了什么？

    [选项]A. We should spend more time growing food.   我们应该花更多的时间种植粮食。B. It's useful to speak at the libraries and schools.   在图书馆和学校演讲很有用。C. It's worth gardening together though it's hard work.   尽管种植很辛苦，但还是值得一起做的。

Step 2: 【回原文，找答案】

14. 文章第一段中Kendall提到，My favourite thing about growing food is doing it with my family and friends.（关于种植食物我最喜欢的事情是和家人朋友一起

做。）故正确答案为A。

15. 文章第二段中，Kendall的奶奶告诉她，Don't throw away the small ones, because if you put them in the ground, they will grow back.（不要扔掉小土豆，因为如果你把它们埋在地里，它们会重新长出来。）B选项中的plant them in the ground指代的就是原文中的put them in the ground，故选B。

16. 文章第三段中提到，My friends help me water and care for the plants.（我的朋友们帮助我浇水和照顾植物。）原文中的water and care for就有"照料"的意思，和A选项中的take care of意思相同，故选A。

17. 文章第四段提到，At the age of six, she became the youngest licensed farmer in Georgia.（在六岁时，她成为佐治亚州最年轻的持照农民。）故本题选B。

18. 文章最后一句话Growing food takes a lot of work, but together you can do it. 意思是，"种植食物需要做很多工作，但只要大家共同努力，就能做到。"由此得知，Kendall认为这样做是值得的，故选C。

【Answer key】

14. A   15. B   16. A   17. B   18. C

Day 6 休闲爱好·考点锦囊

 考点锦囊

1. 在描述"休闲爱好"的文章中，常会提到关于兴趣爱好、休闲活动的相关内容，与其相关的单词或短语如下。

兴趣爱好 — 体育	
snowboarding 滑雪板运动	gymnastics 体操
ice-hockey 冰上曲棍球	rugby 英式橄榄球
skateboarding 滑板运动	sailing 帆船运动
surfboard 冲浪板	horse-riding 骑马
marathon 马拉松赛跑	jogging 慢跑锻炼
racket 球拍	cricket 板球运动

续表

兴趣爱好 — 体育	
dive 潜水	windsurf 风帆冲浪
boxing 拳击	track 跑道

其他兴趣爱好及相关描述	
board game 棋类游戏	puzzle 拼图游戏
hike 远足	climbing 爬山
join... club 加入……俱乐部	attractive 吸引人的
choose 选择	collect 收集
crazy 狂热的	enjoy 享受，喜爱
habit 习惯	membership 会员身份
prefer 更喜欢	swing 秋千

2. 在表达自己对各类休闲活动的态度时，常会用到的短语或句子如下。

✓ get bored of doing sth. 厌倦做某事

✓ be good at... 擅长……

✓ keep sth. interesting for sb. 某事使某人感兴趣

✓ My favourite thing is... 我最喜欢的事情是……

✓ I think... was amazing. 我觉得……很棒。

✓ It is difficult for sb. to do sth. 做某事对某人来说很难

✓ I couldn't believe... 我简直难以相信……

🎧 百变演练

I. Complete the sentences with the correct form of the given words. 用所给单词正确形式补全句子。

1. Kendall spends a lot of time _____ (play) in the earth.

2. Don't _____ (throw) away the small ones.

3. When friends came over, Kendall enjoyed _____ (share) what she knew.

4. At the age of six, she became the _____ (young) licensed farmer in Georgia.

5. People who don't have enough food _____ (invite) to take what they need.

II. Translate. 翻译。

1. She has a huge garden that produces over 100 pounds of food each year!

   _____

2. Kendall tried it and was amazed when the small potatoes grew new leaves.

   _____

3. Soon after, her parents put in a small yard garden.

   _____

4. Kendall is a role model for other children.

   _____

5. Growing food takes a lot of work, but together you can do it.

   _____

III. Read the article of Day 5 and write T or F. 阅读Day 5的文章，并判断正误。

( ) 1. Kendall started gardening when she was six years old.

( ) 2. Kendall's favourite part about gardening is growing food with her family and friends.

( ) 3. Kendall's garden produces less than 100 pounds of food each year.

( ) 4. Kendall is the youngest licensed farmer in Georgia.

( ) 5. Kendall only sells the vegetables and fruits from her garden to make money.

Weekend 三 每周一练

I. Complete the questions with the correct question word(s). 用正确的疑问词补全问题。

1. _____ do they go to the movies? Once a month.

2. _____ did you go on vacation last summer? I went to London.

3. _____ will we see you again?

4. _____ does your sister usually do after school?

5. _____ were you late? I want to know the reason.

II. Put the words into the correct order to make sentences and questions. 连词成句。

1. he / dance / Why / club / did / the / join / ?

_____

2. did / moving / about / feel / How / she / school / new / a / to / ?

_____

3. sorry / He / didn't / harder / is / he / try / .

_____

4. signs / trail / There / more / along / the / should / be / .

_____

5. breakfast / already / finished / have / I / my / .

_____

III. Read and choose the correct answer for each question. 阅读文章，选择正确答案。

J.B. Gill

Ten years ago, J. B. Gill moved from the city to start his own farm. As one of the members of a pop group, Gill had lived a busy life but the farm gave him a way to relax.

Although farming was new to him, Gill took the challenge and his experiences helped him write his book *Ace and the Animal Heroes*. The story follows Ace, whose life changes greatly when he moves to the countryside. After trying on a pair of magical boots, Ace realizes he can speak to the animals, who make up their minds to protect the farm.

Gill says that if he had his own pair of magical boots, he would love to speak to wildlife, especially the wild deer that sometimes appear near his farm. As they have no owners, Gill feels like he's sharing their home. "It's really interesting to hear what they're thinking and know where they're at," he said.

Gill got his ideas for writing from the animals on his family farm. His children, Ace and Chiara, helped out with his book. Together, Gill's family made sure that the pictures in the book looked like the animals they'd been based on. He said, "All of those have been really great to piece the whole book together."

1. What did Gill decide to do ten years ago?

   A. Write a new book.

   B. Start his own farm.

   C. Move to the city.

2. How did Ace's life change in the story?

   A. He became a pop star.

   B. He moved to the city.

   C. He discovered he could talk to animals.

3. What can we learn about Gill from paragraph 3?

   A. He cares about wildlife.

   B. He develops many interests.

   C. He was born with magic.

4. Where did Gill get the idea for his book?

   A. From his group members.

   B. From his children's pictures.

   C. From the animals on the farm.

5. What did Ace and Chiara contribute to J. B. Gill's book?

   A. They helped with the writing process.

   B. They provided ideas for the story.

   C. They helped with the pictures.

Week 6 完形填空题

考试模块	时间	主题	内容	
		第6周目标		
	Day 1	威廉·珀金	William Perkin	☐
	Day 2	度假地莫纳岛	Mona Island	☐
Part 4 完形填空题	Day 3	可爱的松鼠	Cute Squirrels	☐
	Day 4	伊萨克·牛顿	Issac Newton	☐
	Day 5	神奇的大自然	Amazing Nature	☐
	Weekend	每周一练	模拟训练	☐

Day 1　威廉·珀金

 考场模拟

For each question, choose the correct answer.

William Perkin

William Perkin was born in London in 1838. As a child he had many hobbies, including model making and photography. But it was the (19) _____ of chemistry that really interested him. At the age of 15, he went to college to study it.

While he was there, he was (20) _____ to make a medicine from coal. This didn't go well, but when he was working on the problem, he found a cheap (21) _____ to make the colour purple.

At that (22) _____ it was very expensive to make clothes in different colours. William knew he could make a business out of his new colour. Helped by his father and brother, William (23) _____ his own factory to make the colour. It sold well, and soon purple clothes (24) _____ very popular in England and the rest of the world.

19 A. class   B. subject   C. course

20 A. thinking   B. trying   C. deciding

21 A. way   B. path   C. plan

22 A. day   B. time   C. hour

23 A. brought   B. turned   C. opened

24 A. began   B. arrived   C. became

 ## 思路点拨

Step 1：【读文章，知大意】

1. 文章主旨

   这篇文章主要介绍了威廉·珀金的故事，他通过研究化学，成功发现了制作紫色染料的廉价方法，从而开创了化学染料工业。

2. 考点　考查名词辨析和动词辨析。

Step 2：【找线索，选答案】

19.【考点】名词辨析

【解析】A选项class意为"班级"，B选项subject意为"学科；科目"，C选项course意为"课程"。关键词为空格后的chemistry（化学），为一门学科，且句意为"但他真正感兴趣的是化学学科。"故选B。

20.【考点】动词辨析

【解析】A选项thinking意为"认为"，B选项trying意为"试图"，C选项deciding意为"决定"。关键词为空格后的to make，think后不能加to do，故排除A；decide 常不用于进行时，故排除C；try to do sth. 表示"试图做某事"。故选B。

21.【考点】名词辨析

【解析】A选项way意为"方法"，B选项path意为"小路"，C选项plan意为"计划"。根据句意"这并不顺利，但当他在解决这个问题时，他找到了一种廉价的_____来制作紫色。"可知A符合，find a way to do sth. 表示"找到做某事的方法"。故选A。

22.【考点】名词辨析

【解析】A选项day意为"天"，B选项time意为"时间"，C选项hour意为"小时"。at that time为固定搭配，表示"那时候"。句意为"在那个时候，制作不同颜色的衣服非常昂贵。"故选B。

23.【考点】动词辨析

【解析】A选项brought意为"带来"，B选项turned意为"变成"，C选项opened意为"开张，开业"。关键词为空格后的his own factory，结合句意"在父亲和兄弟的帮助下，威廉_____自己的工厂生产这种颜色。"可知C符合，opened his own factory意为"开自己的工厂"。故选C。

24.【考点】动词辨析

【解析】A选项began意为"开始"，B选项arrived意为"到达"，C选项became意为"开始变得"。关键词为空格后的popular，为形容词，分析句子成分可知，空格处应填系动词，系动词后面可以接形容词，故排除A和B。become后可以接形容词，became very popular意为"变得非常流行"，句意为"它卖得很好，很快紫色衣服就在英国和世界其他地方流行起来。"故选C。

【Answer key】

| 19. B | 20. B | 21. A | 22. B | 23. C | 24. C |

🎧 考点锦囊

有关"名人介绍"的文章中，常会涉及一些关于成长经历的话题，与其相关的单词或短语如下。

成长经历	
childhood 童年	relationship 关系
teenager 青少年	family 家庭
adulthood 成年	parents 父母
development 发展	sibling 兄弟姐妹
experience 经历	friend 朋友
challenge 挑战	hobby 爱好

成长经历	
milestone 里程碑	interest 兴趣
learning 学习	passion 热情
growth 成长	dream 梦想
maturity 成熟	aspiration 抱负
education 教育	values 价值
college 大学	principle 原则
degree 学位	habit 习惯
job 工作	pattern 模式
profession 职业	lifestyle 生活方式
work experience 工作经验	choice 选择
outcome 结果	decision 决定

 百变演练

Choose the correct answer to complete the sentence. 选择正确答案填空。（名词辨析）

1. —Tara, what's your favourite _____ ?

   —Orange. Half of my dresses are orange.

   A. fruit   B. drink   C. colour

2. How much _____ do we need to make a banana milk shake?

   A. bananas   B. apples   C. milk

3. Lucy's father works in No. 2 Hospital. He is a _____ .

   A. teacher   B. doctor   C. policeman

4. I don't know how to make a speech in public. Can you give me some _____ ?

   A. water   B. food   C. advice

5. It is a good _____ to take a school bus because it's quite safe.

   A. risk   B. choice   C. game

Day 2 　度假地莫纳岛

 考场模拟

For each question, choose the correct answer.

Mona Island

Mona Island is an amazing place to take a vacation. Some of the animals living there can't be (19) _____ anywhere else in the world. There are fascinating beaches and caves to explore. The sea around the island has colourful fishes.

(20) _____ can come to the island to have a close look at many kinds of fishes. They can dive far below the surface. They use special tools to be able to breathe under the water. Through the clear water, they can see the (21) _____ of the fishes.

After a full day of fun activities, visitors can take a (22) _____ , listen to the night sounds, and watch the stars in the huge (23) _____ . The stars are easier to (24) _____ . Visitors say that watching the stars is amazing. It's the perfect end to a perfect day.

19 A. told   B. found   C. sold

20 A. Visitors   B. Farmers   C. Neighbours

21 A. cotton   B. collar   C. colours

22 A. race   B. stop   C. rest

23 A. sky   B. ground   C. land

24 A. touch   B. see   C. catch

 思路点拨

Step 1:【读文章，知大意】

1. 文章主旨

   这篇文章主要介绍了莫纳岛作为一个绝佳的度假胜地，拥有独特的动物、迷人的海滩和洞穴，以及丰富多彩的海洋生物。

2. 考点　考查名词辨析和动词辨析。

Step 2:【找线索，选答案】

19.【考点】动词辨析

【解析】A选项意为"告诉"，B选项意为"发现，找到"，C选项意为"卖"。根据句意"生活在那里的一些动物在世界其他任何地方都找不到。"可知B符合，found是find的过去分词形式，意为"发现，找到"。故选B。

20.【考点】名词辨析

【解析】A选项意为"游客"，B选项意为"农民"，C选项意为"邻居"。文章开头提到"莫纳岛是一个度假的好地方。"所以空格处应该填入表示"游客"的词。句意为"游客可以来岛上近距离观察各种各样的鱼。"故选A。

21.【考点】名词辨析

【解析】A选项意为"棉"，B选项意为"衣领"，C选项意为"颜色"。关键词为空格前的the clear water，意为"清澈的水"，由此可知C符合。句意为"透过清澈的水，他们可以看到鱼的颜色。"故选C。

22.【考点】名词辨析

【解析】A选项意为"比赛"，B选项作名词时意为"车站"，C选项意为"休息"。take a rest为固定搭配，表示"休息一下"，等于have a rest。句意为"经过一整天的有趣活动后，游客可以休息一下……"，故选C。

23.【考点】名词辨析

【解析】A选项意为"天空"，B选项意为"地面"，C选项意为"陆地"。关键词为空格后的watch the stars，意为"看星星"，由此可知A符合。句意为"……看着浩瀚天空中的星星。"故选A。

24.【考点】动词辨析

【解析】A选项意为"触摸"，B选项意为"看"，C选项意为"抓住"。关键词为空格前的star，意为"星星"，天空中的星星可以"看"，但不能"触摸"或"抓住"。句意为"星星更容易看到。"故选B。

【Answer key】

| 19. B | 20. A | 21. C | 22. C | 23. A | 24. B |

🎧 **考点锦囊**

有关"景点介绍"的文章中，常会涉及一些关于自然景观、建筑特色、文化古迹等话题，与其相关的单词或短语如下。

自然景观

mountain 山	desert 沙漠
lake 湖泊	forest 森林
sea 大海	grassland 草原
waterfall 瀑布	gorge 峡谷
river 河流	cave 洞穴

建筑特色

palace 宫殿	garden 园林
castle 城堡	ancient architecture 古代建筑
temple 寺庙	modern architecture 现代建筑
church 教堂	folk house 民居

文化古迹

site 遗址	stone carving 石雕
tomb 古墓	relics 文物
mural 壁画	historical relics 历史遗迹

百变演练

Choose the correct answer to complete the sentence. 选择正确答案填空。（动词辨析）

1. —Why don't you _____ up smoking? It's very harmful.

   —I tried many times, but it's really hard.

   A. give   B. ring   C. put

2. My aunt offered me a dictionary and I _____ it happily.

   A. accepted   B. invited   C. grew

3. _____ me, I'll show you the way.

   A. Follow   B. Forget   C. Leave

4.　—Why didn't you go to my party last night?

　　—Sorry, I was _____ for the English test at that time.

　　A. caring 　　　　　　 B. looking 　　　　　　 C. studying

5.　He thanked me for _____ out the mistakes in his homework.

　　A. going 　　　　　　 B. pointing 　　　　　　 C. putting

Day 3 　可爱的松鼠

🎧 考场模拟

For each question, choose the correct answer.

Cute Squirrels

Squirrels are cute and interesting animals that can be found in (19) _____ parts of the world. They are known for their long tails, (20) _____ teeth, and the ability to climb trees.

They can jump up to 6 metres (21) _____ , and they can run up to 32 kilometres every hour.

Squirrels are known for their love of nuts, and they can (22) _____ as much food as their body weight each week. They will often (23) _____ nuts in the ground for the long winter months.

One funny thing is that squirrels are (24) _____ at planting trees. They hide the fruits of oak trees, but often forget where they put them. In the end, the forgotten fruits become big trees.

19	A. lots	B. many	C. much
20	A. old	B. big	C. great
21	A. large	B. high	C. long
22	A. eat	B. drink	C. plant
23	A. belong	B. lend	C. keep
24	A. good	B. hard	C. nice

思路点拨

Step 1:【读文章，知大意】

1. 文章主旨

这篇文章主要介绍了松鼠的特点和习性，包括它们的可爱外貌、长尾巴、锋利牙齿以及爬树能力，还有它们对坚果的热爱以及埋藏果实的能力。

2. 考点　考查限定词辨析、形容词辨析和动词辨析。

Step 2:【找线索，选答案】

19.【考点】限定词辨析

【解析】A选项意为"大量，许多"，常与of连用，lots of=a lot of，意为"许多"；B选项意为"许多"，后面接可数名词；C选项意为"许多"，后面接不可数名词。关键词为空格后的parts，意为"区域，地区"，为可数名词。故选B。

20.【考点】形容词辨析

【解析】A选项意为"老的，年纪大的"；B选项意为"大的"，强调体积、程度、数量等大的；C选项意为"大的"，多指数量大，常与量词连用，比如，a great amount of（大量）、a great number of（许多）。关键词为空格后的teeth，意为"牙齿"，teeth是tooth的复数形式。句意为"它们以长尾巴、大牙齿和爬树能力而闻名。"故选B。

21.【考点】形容词辨析

【解析】A选项意为"大的"，B选项意为"高的"，C选项意为"长的"。关键词为空格前的jump up to 6 metres，意为"跳到6米"，由此可知B符合。句意为"它们能跳到6米高，每小时能跑到32公里。"故选B。

22.【考点】动词辨析

【解析】A选项意为"吃"，B选项意为"喝；饮"，C选项意为"种植"。关键词为空格后的food，意为"食物"，由此可知A符合，eat food意为"进食"。句意为"松鼠是出了名的爱吃坚果，它们每周能吃掉和自己体重一样多的食物。"故选A。

23.【考点】动词辨析

【解析】A选项意为"属于"，常与to连用，belong to意为"属于"；B选项意为"借"，常用于lend sth. to sb. 或 lend sb. sth.，意为"把某物借给某人"；C选项意为"保持；存放"。根据空格后的nuts in the ground，可知C符合，keep取"存放"之意。句意为"在漫长的冬季，它们经常把坚果存放在地里。"故选C。

24.【考点】形容词辨析

【解析】A选项意为"好的"，B选项意为"困难的"，C选项意为"美好的"。be good at为固定搭配，表示"擅长于"。句意为"一件有趣的事情是松鼠很擅长植树。"故选A。

【Answer key】

19. B	20. B	21. B	22. A	23. C	24. A

🎧 考点锦囊

有关"动植物"的文章中，常会涉及一些关于动物、植物、生长和发育等话题，与其相关的单词或短语如下。

动物	
cat 猫	rabbit 兔子
dog 狗	lion 狮子
bird 鸟	tiger 老虎
fish 鱼	insect 昆虫
bee 蜜蜂	butterfly 蝴蝶

植物水果	
flower 花	grape 葡萄
tree 树	leaf 叶子
grass 草	seed 种子
apple 苹果	fruit 果实
banana 香蕉	root 根

生长发育	
grow 生长	adult 成年
germinate 发芽	life cycle 生命周期

续表

生长发育	
bloom 开花	grow 生长，发育
bear fruit 结果	hatch 孵化
cub 幼崽	young animal 幼小的动物

🎧 百变演练

Choose the correct answer to complete the sentence. 选择正确答案填空。（形容词和副词辨析）

1. I like these books because they offer me a lot of _____ knowledge.

   A. useful   B. boring   C. useless

2. —What is your new classmate like?

   —She is very shy. She speaks so _____ that I can hardly hear her.

   A. loudly   B. clearly   C. quietly

3. What a _____ boy! He worked out such a difficult math problem.

   A. clever   B. kind   C. lazy

4. —Which is_____, the blue one or the red one?

   —The blue one.

   A. good   B. better   C. best

5. Photos speak _____, but they say a lot about our lives.

   A. quickly   B. bravely   C. silently

Day 4   伊萨克·牛顿

🎧 考场模拟

For each question, choose the correct answer.

Issac Newton

Issac Newton was born in England in 1643. He was a quiet boy. Having lost his father before he was born, he (19) _____ up with his grandparents. At 17, soon after he finished schooling, his mother hoped he could take (20) _____ of their family farm. But instead of watching sheep, young Newton would (21) _____ his time making small tools. His head teacher saw the talent in him and (22) _____ his mother to send him to the university. Newton set out for Cambridge in June, 1661, and (23) _____ his career in scientific research.

Newton was an English physicist. Because of the (24) _____ work Newton has done, he is regarded as one of the greatest scientists of all time.

19 A. drew   B. built   C. grew

20 A. fact   B. part   C. care

21 A. spend   B. bought   C. pay

22 A. asked   B. answered   C. failed

23 A. arrived   B. began   C. became

24 A. important   B. wonderful   C. advanced

思路点拨

Step 1:【读文章，知大意】

1. 文章主旨

   这篇文章主要介绍了英国物理学家艾萨克·牛顿的生平，包括他的童年、成长经历以及他在科学研究方面的杰出成就，他被誉为历史上最伟大的科学家之一。

2. 考点 考查动词辨析、名词辨析和形容词辨析。

Step 2:【找线索，选答案】

19.【考点】动词辨析

【解析】A选项意为"画画"，B选项意为"建造"，C选项意为"生长"。关键词为空格后的up，grow up为固定搭配，表示"长大"。句意为"他在出生前就失去了父亲，和祖父母一起长大。"故选C。

20.【考点】名词辨析

【解析】A选项意为"事实"，B选项意为"部分"，C选项意为"照顾；照料"。take care of为固定搭配，表示"照顾；照料"。句意为"17岁时，他刚毕业不久，母亲就希望他能照料家里的农场。"故选C。

21. 【考点】动词辨析

【解析】A选项意为"花费"，常用表达为spend time in doing sth.，意为"花费时间做某事"；B选项意为"买"；C选项意为"支付"，常用于pay the bill（付账）或pay cash（付现金）。关键词为空格后的his time making，A符合。句意为"但是年轻的牛顿没有去放羊，而是把时间花在制作小工具上。"故选A。

22. 【考点】动词辨析

【解析】A选项意为"询问；要求"，常用ask sb. to do sth.，意为"要求某人做某事"；B选项意为"回答"，常用表达为answer questions（回答问题）；C选项意为"失败"。关键词为空格后的his mother to send，由此可知A符合。句意为"他的班主任看到了他的天赋，让他妈妈送他上大学"，故选A。

23. 【考点】动词辨析

【解析】A选项意为"到达"，B选项意为"开始"，C选项意为"开始变得"。根据句意"1661年6月，牛顿启程前往剑桥，开始了他的科学研究生涯。"可知B符合，故选B。

24. 【考点】形容词辨析

【解析】A选项意为"重要的"，B选项意为"精彩的"，C选项意为"先进的"。关键词为空格后的work，意为"工作"，由此可知A符合，important work意为"重要的工作"。句意为"由于牛顿所做的重要工作，他被认为是有史以来最伟大的科学家之一。"故选A。

【Answer key】

19. C   20. C   21. A   22. A   23. B   24. A

 考点锦囊

有关"名人介绍"的文章中，常会涉及一些关于成就、特点、品质和价值观的话题，与其相关的单词或短语如下。

职业成就	
belief 信仰	leadership 领导力
creativity 创造力	kindness 善良

职业成就	
determination 决心	management 管理
drive 驱动力	maturity 成熟度
enthusiasm 热忱	moral 道德观
excellence 卓越	passion 热情
genius 天才	problem-solver 问题解决者
hardworking 勤奋	responsibility 责任心
impact 影响	responsible 有责任心
achievement 成就	skills 技能
vision 远见	social skills 社交能力
smart 聪明的	success 成功
creative 有创造力的	talent 才能
value 价值	trait 特质

🎧 百变演练

Choose the correct answer to complete the sentence. 选择正确答案填空。（动词辨析）

1. Mom is cooking chicken soup, it _____ so good.

   A. sounds   B. tastes   C. smells

2. I saw Bob in the garden. He _____ flowers there.

   A. waters   B. has watered   C. was watering

3. The trip _____ really exciting to me. How I wish to go!

   A. sounds   B. feels   C. tastes

4. Alice often _____ the fun of doing DIY with us. She is so creative!

   A. shares   B. gives   C. makes

5. Last Sunday my brother and I _____ our grandparents.

   A. visits   B. visited   C. visit

Day 5 神奇的大自然

 考场模拟

For each question, choose the correct answer.

Amazing Nature

Nature is amazing! Did you know how butterflies (19) _____ the flying insects? It's one of the amazing wonders of nature.

In the beginning, butterflies (20) _____ a small egg on a leaf of a plant.

It's hard to believe that the egg will become something (21) _____ in a few days. It becomes a walking insect. This insect is (22) _____ caterpillar.

Soon, after growing big, the caterpillar makes a cover for itself.

After a period of time, the cover breaks and a wet, weak butterfly appears. Shortly, the beautiful, colourful butterfly spreads its wings and (23) _____ away.

This is just one (24) _____ of the wonders of nature. Look around the natural world, and you will learn many really amazing things.

19 A. begin	B. become	C. come
20 A. lay	B. lie	C. dig
21 A. wrong	B. important	C. different
22 A. collected	B. called	C. decided
23 A. forget	B. cries	C. flies
24 A. example	B. excuse	C. failure

思路点拨

Step 1:【读文章，知大意】

    1. 文章主旨

        这篇文章主要介绍了蝴蝶的生命周期，包括从卵到毛毛虫再到蝴蝶的过程，展现了自然界的奇妙和美丽。

2. 考点　考查动词辨析、名词辨析和形容词辨析。

Step 2:【找线索，选答案】

19.【考点】动词辨析

【解析】A选项意为"开始"，B选项意为"变成"，C选项意为"来"。关键词为空格前后的butterflies（蝴蝶）和the flying insects（会飞的昆虫），可知B符合。句意为"你知道蝴蝶是怎样变成飞虫的吗?"故选B。

20.【考点】动词辨析

【解析】A选项意为"下（蛋），产（卵）"，B选项意为"躺；说谎"，C选项意为"挖"。关键词为空格后的egg，意为"蛋；卵"，表示"下蛋，产卵"，要用lay an egg。句意为"起初，蝴蝶在植物的叶子上产下小卵。"故选A。

21.【考点】形容词辨析

【解析】A选项意为"错误的"，B选项意为"重要的"，C选项意为"不同的"。根据上下文可知，蝴蝶起初是卵，后来变成了会爬的昆虫，由此可知空格处应填表示"不同的"的词。句意为"很难相信这颗卵在几天内就会变成不同的东西。它变成了会爬的昆虫。"故选C。

22.【考点】动词辨析

【解析】A选项意为"收集"，B选项意为"把……叫作"，C选项意为"决定"。根据上文，可知此处句意为"这种昆虫叫作毛毛虫。"故选B。

23.【考点】动词辨析

【解析】A选项意为"忘记"，B选项意为"哭泣"，C选项意为"飞"。关键词为空格后的away，fly away为固定短语，意为"飞走"，C符合，A和B后不能接away。句意为"不一会儿，那只美丽多彩的蝴蝶展开翅膀飞走了。"故选C。

24.【考点】名词辨析

【解析】A选项意为"例子"，B选项意为"借口；理由"，C选项意为"失败"。根据上下文句意"这只是大自然奇迹的一个_____。看看自然界，你会学到很多令人惊奇的东西。"可知A符合，one example of the wonders of nature意为"大自然奇迹的一个例子"。故选A。

【Answer key】

19. B　　20. A　　21. C　　22. B　　23. C　　24. A

考点锦囊

有关"自然环境"的文章中，常会涉及一些关于自然、环境、栖息地等话题，与其相关的单词或短语如下。

自然环境	
air 空气	nature 自然
forest 森林	plant 植物
climate 气候	tree 树木
desert 沙漠	water 水
ecosystem 生态系统	soil 土壤
environment 环境	temperature 温度
flowers 花	wetland 湿地
grassland 草原	habitat 栖息地
insect 昆虫	natural condition 自然条件

百变演练

Choose the correct answer to complete the sentence. 选择正确答案填空。（名词辨析）

1. —Hello! May I speak to Tony, please?

   — Sorry, I'm afraid you have the wrong _____.

   A. telephone   B. name   C. number

2. If the weather is nice, we could have a(n) _____ in the park.

   A. picnic   B. chance   C. place

3. His beautiful music has brought _____ to people all over the world.

   A. danger   B. pleasure   C. weather

4. Your leg looks really bad! I think you should send for a _____ about that.

   A. pilot   B. doctor   C. singer

5. My uncle works in a hospital, and he is a _____.

   A. doctors   B. nurses   C. doctor

Weekend 三 每周一练

I. Circle the correct word to complete each sentence. 圈出正确的单词补全句子。

1. On a **dark / clear** day, you can see most of the city from the top of the tower.

2. Cindy felt **lonely / cold** in her new school, so she joined some clubs to make new friends.

3. The new restaurant is **awful / exciting**. We waited a long time for the food to arrive.

4. I only got four hours of sleep last night, so I feel **tired / hungry** today.

5. Although he failed many times, he **often / never** gave up his dream.

6. High-speed trains are much **fast / faster** than traditional ones.

7. Sue works **alone / carefully**, so she never seems to make mistakes.

8. It is **polite / rude** to say "thank you" very often, even to family members.

II. Choose the correct answer to complete the sentence. 选择正确答案填空。

1. —I do morning exercises every day.

    —It's a good habit. It helps you keep in good _____ .

    A. time   B. touch   C. health

2. It's raining heavily. Please take the _____ .

    A. stone   B. flower   C. umbrella

3. Which ice cream do you want, Mary? You can't have all of them. You have to make

    a _____ .

    A. wish   B. call   C. choice

4. —Jack, I have no idea for the report.

    —Me neither. Why don't we ask the teacher for _____ ?

    A. help   B. tickets   C. food

5. The hat is not the right _____ for me. I'd like a smaller one.

    A. size   B. style   C. colour

6. Put _____ first and be careful while riding on the road!

    A. interest   B. money   C. safety

III. Complete the sentences with the words in the box. 用框中的单词补全句子。

| sounds | drawing | turn | get | borrowed | point |

1. It's impolite to _____ at anyone with your chopsticks.

2. Sam _____ a computer from me yesterday.

3. Your idea _____ good. Let's give it a try and see if it will work.

4. Jim is going to join the Art Club because he likes _____.

5. —Kate, don't forget to _____ off the light when you leave the room.

   —OK, mom.

6. I _____ up at 6 a.m. so I can leave for school at 7 a.m.

IV. Read and choose the correct sentences to complete the conversation. 读一读，选择正确的句子补全对话。

A: Tom, could you help me?

B: Fine. _____ 1 _____

A: Take out the rubbish, please.

B: No problem. _____ 2 _____

A: To the rubbish bins around the street corner.

B: OK. I'll go at once!

A: _____ 3 _____

B: How many bins are there?

A: _____ 4 _____

B: But how can I know which is the right one?

A: It's easy to tell. They have different colours and signs.

B: _____ 5 _____

A. OK. I see.   B. There are four.

C. You can do many things.   D. But where should I take it?

E. What do you want me to do?   F. What colour is the rubbish bin?

G. Don't forget to put it in the right bin.

V. Complete the sentences according to the Chinese meanings. 根据中文提示，完成句子。

1. 加入社团是一个很好的交友方式。

   Joining a club is a good way to _____ _____.

2. 每日练习对学习英语来说很重要。

   It's _____ to _____ English every day.

3. 我们将一起努力实现梦想。

   We'll work together to make our dreams _____ _____.

4. 书读得越多，你懂得就越多。

   The _____ books you read, the _____ you'll know.

5. 努力地工作是重要的，但我们也必须有时间放松。

   It is important to _____ _____ but we must also have time to relax.

VI. Complete the sentences with the correct form of the words. 用所给单词的适当形式补全句子。

1. Our home is the _____ (three) from the end on the left.

2. My teacher always offers us help _____ (patient).

3. You're expected _____ (shake) hands when meeting people for the first time in China.

4. I _____ (learn) English ever since I was five years old.

5. Frank has more than 500 _____ (stamp).

6. Let me _____ (tell) you about my favourite book.

语法填空题

Day 1　假期游玩

 考场模拟

For each question, write the correct answer.

Write one word for each gap.

Example:	**0**	you

From:	Maria
To:	Lliy

I hope **(0)** _____ are well. I'm having a great holiday here in Thailand. Our hotel is very nice and there are a lot of good restaurants near it.

Yesterday morning, we went to **(25)** _____ lovely beach. We had to leave before lunch because it was very hot. We went to a party **(26)** _____ the evening in the centre **(27)** _____ the town. Everyone had a good time and we got back at midnight. Tomorrow, we want to **(28)** _____ on a boat trip or **(29)** _____ tennis. I'll show you my photos **(30)** _____ I get back.

See you soon,

Maria

思路点拨

Step 1:【读文章，知大意】

1. 文章主旨

   这是一篇Maria写给Lliy的邮件，主要介绍了Maria在泰国度假的情况，包括酒店和附近的美食，以及昨天早上去海滩的经历和晚上的派对。她提到明天计划去乘船旅行，并表示要分享照片。

2. 考点 考查冠词、代词、介词、连词和固定搭配。

Step 2:【找线索，填答案】

25.【考点】冠词或代词

   【解析】根据句意"昨天早上，我们去了一个美丽的海滩。"beach为名词，前面可用冠词a或代词this修饰。"一个美丽的海滩"为泛指，用冠词a。this lovely beach意为"这个美丽的海滩"，表示双方都知道的某个海滩。

26.【考点】介词

   【解析】表示"在晚上"，通常用介词in，类似的还有in the morning（在早上）、in the afternoon（在下午）。根据句意"我们晚上去市中心参加了一个聚会。"此处也可填during（在……期间），during the evening意为"在晚上期间"。故正确答案为in或during。

27.【考点】介词

   【解析】根据句意"城镇的中心"，表示"……的"，可以用介词of，即of the town（城镇的）。故正确答案为of。

28.【考点】固定搭配

   【解析】题目中提到了on a boat trip，表示要坐船旅行，go on a boat trip是固定搭配，表示"坐船旅行"。故正确答案为go。

29.【考点】固定搭配

【解析】题目中提到了tennis，表示要"打网球"或"观看网球比赛"。play tennis是固定搭配，表示"打网球"。watch tennis表示"观看网球比赛"。故正确答案为play或watch。

30.【考点】连词

【解析】该句中，"I'll show you my photos _____ I get back"是一个时间状语从句，要用连词来引导。根据句意，可以考虑使用after或when。after表示"在……之后"，after I get back可以表达"在我回来之后给你看照片"的意思。when表示"当……的时候"，when I get back也可以表达"当我回来的时候给你看照片"的意思。故正确答案为when或after。

【Answer key】

25. a / this　　26. in / during　　27. of　　28. go　　29. play / watch　　30. when / after

🎧 考点锦囊

描述假期或与假期相关的活动或事件，考生要掌握的词组或搭配如下。

<table>
<tr><td colspan="2" align="center">冠词、介词相关表达</td></tr>
<tr><td>a three-day holiday 三天的假期</td><td>the winter skiing trip 冬季滑雪之旅</td></tr>
<tr><td>on holiday 在度假</td><td>during a road trip 在公路旅行中</td></tr>
<tr><td>during the summer vacation 在暑假期间</td><td>in the city centre 在市中心</td></tr>
<tr><td>on the weekend 在周末</td><td>at the amusement park 在游乐园</td></tr>
<tr><td>at the beach 在海滩上</td><td>in the national park 在国家公园</td></tr>
<tr><td>by the pool 在泳池旁</td><td>by the lakefront 在湖边</td></tr>
<tr><td>in the mountains 在山区</td><td>on the sandy beach 在沙滩上</td></tr>
<tr><td>on the slopes 在（雪）坡上</td><td>at the ski resort 在滑雪胜地</td></tr>
<tr><td>at the resort 在度假村</td><td>by the sea 在海边</td></tr>
<tr><td>in the countryside 在乡村地区</td><td>by the bonfire 在篝火旁</td></tr>
</table>

🎧 **百变演练**

Choose the correct answer to complete the sentence. 选择正确答案填空。（冠词）

1. After _____ school, I bought _____ present for my mother.

   A. /; a   B. a; /   C. a; the

2. —Are you free on weekends?

   —Yes, I am going to have _____ picnic on _____ Sunday.

   A. the; an   B. a; the   C. a; /

3. There is _____ bank across from the hospital.

   A. a   B. an   C. the

4. As we know, Singapore is _____ Asian country.

   A. a   B. an   C. the

5. My brother often plays _____ football with his classmates after school.

   A. a   B. an   C. /

Day 2   班级旅行

🎧 **考场模拟**

For each question, write the correct answer.

Write one word for each gap.

Example:	**0**	you

From:	Eliza
To:	Mum and Dad

I hope **(0)** _____ are well. The class trip was fun, **(25)** _____ the journey from school took a long time.

On **(26)** _____ way, we went to a museum about the history of the area. It **(27)** _____ quite interesting. We were all tired when we finally arrived here.

I am in the same room with three friends. We have **(28)** _____ keep our room tidy, which is difficult at times! The teachers come to check our rooms **(29)** _____ we go to bed.

I emailed you **(30)** _____ photos and I'm sure you'll like them—they're so funny.

Lots of love,

Eliza

思路点拨

Step 1:【读文章，知大意】

1. 文章主旨

这是一篇Eliza写给父母的邮件，主要介绍了Eliza参加班级旅行的情况，包括旅途中的经历、到达目的地后的感受、与朋友共住的房间的情况以及发送照片的事情。

2. 考点 考查连词、冠词、动词、连词、限定词和固定搭配。

Step 2:【找线索，填答案】

25.【考点】连词

【解析】根据句意"班级旅行很有趣，_____从学校出发的路程花了很长时间。"前后两个句子之间为转折关系，因此应该用连词but。

26.【考点】冠词或固定搭配

【解析】on the way是固定短语，意为"在路上"。故正确答案为the。

27.【考点】动词

【解析】主语是it（指博物馆），空格后为quite interesting（非常有趣），所以空格处要填单数形式的be动词，而该段陈述的是已经发生过的事情，因此应该用be动词的过去式was。故正确答案为was。

28.【考点】固定搭配

【解析】根据上下文可知，这句话的意思是"我们必须保持房间整洁。"其中表示"必须"用固定短语have to。故正确答案为to。

29.【考点】连词

【解析】根据句意"老师来检查我们的房间_____我们上床睡觉。"两者为时间上的先后顺序，"老师来检查我们的房间"发生在"我们上床睡觉"之前，因此要用before表示"在……之前"。故正确答案为before。

30.【考点】限定词

【解析】关键词photos（照片）为可数名词复数。根据句意"我通过电子邮件给你们发了_____照片，我相信你们会喜欢的——它们真的很有趣。"可知此处应该填表示"许多"的词，故正确答案为some或many。

【Answer key】

25. but   26. the   27. was   28. to   29. before   30. some / many

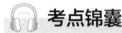

考点锦囊

描述学校学习相关的活动或事件，考生要掌握的词组或搭配如下。

介词相关表达	
in the school 在学校里	in the cafeteria 在自助餐厅里
in the classroom 在教室里	at the study group 在学习小组中
in the learning centre 在学习中心	in the class discussion 在课堂讨论中
at the school gate 在学校门口	after school 放学后
on the blackboard 在黑板上	in the student council 在学生会中
in the library 在图书馆里	at the book fair 在书展上
at the computer lab 在计算机实验室	in the exam hall 在考试大厅里
in the science lab 在科学实验室	on the playground 在操场上
at the schoolyard 在校园里	in the student union 在学生会中
at the graduation ceremony 在毕业典礼上	

百变演练

Choose the correct answer to complete the sentence. 选择正确答案填空。（介词）

1. — How do you relax in your free time?

   — _____ doing sports and listening to music.

   A. At   B. By   C. In

2. Mingming will have a class meeting _____ 3:30 this afternoon.

   A. on   B. in   C. at

3. The traffic light is green. Let's go _____ the road.

   A. against   B. above   C. across

4. _____ spring, the days are often windy and bright. It's a perfect time to fly a kite.

   A. On   B. In   C. At

5. Many thanks _____ your gift. I love it.

   A. in   B. of   C. for

Day 3   特殊节日

 考场模拟

For each question, write the correct answer.

Write one word for each gap.

Example:	**0**	for

From:	Amy
To:	Sam

Thanks **(0)** _____ your letter. It was nice to hear **(25)** _____ you again. So you would like to know what is a special time where I live.

In my hometown, I think **(26)** _____ most important day is the first day of the Spring Festival when we welcome the new year. First, we have dumplings for breakfast. There are coins in breakfast and the people who get **(27)** _____ will have good luck.

(28) _____ breakfast, we visit relatives and play games. Some people go around houses, playing music, and people give them money. In **(29)** _____ evening, there **(30)** _____ fireworks in the town square to say goodbye to winter. Some people wear costumes and dance. Do you celebrate a special day in your country?

思路点拨

Step 1:【读文章，知大意】

1. 文章主旨

   这是一篇Amy回复Sam的邮件，主要介绍了Amy所在家乡的春节，包括早餐、拜访亲戚、游戏、音乐和烟花等庆祝活动。

2. 考点　考查冠词、代词、连词、最高级、固定搭配和固定句型。

Step 2:【找线索，填答案】

25.【考点】固定搭配

【解析】根据句意"很高兴再次收到你的来信。"表示"收到某人的来信"，用hear from sb.。故正确答案为from。

26.【考点】最高级

【解析】关键词most important day（最重要的一天）为形容词最高级用法，形容词最高级前要加the。该句意为"我认为最重要的日子是春节的第一天，当我们迎接新年的时候。"故正确答案为the。

27.【考点】代词

【解析】根据句意"早餐里有硬币，得到硬币的人会有好运气。"可以确定此处要填写一个代词来代替前文提到的coins。get是动词，后面缺少宾语，所以用代词的宾格形式them。故正确答案为them。

28.【考点】连词

【解析】上文提到了"吃早餐"，所以下文应该表示早餐之后发生的事情，此处应该填写表示时间顺序的连词after，after breakfast意为"早餐后"。位于句首，首字母大写。故正确答案为After。

29.【考点】冠词

【解析】in the evening为固定短语，表示"在晚上"。故正确答案为the。

30.【考点】固定句型

【解析】此处句意为"晚上，小镇广场上放烟花，向冬天告别。"分析句子结构可知，此句是there be结构，空格后的fireworks是可数名词复数形式，be动词要用复数形式。故正确答案为are。

25. from   26. the   27. them   28. After   29. the   30. are

考点锦囊

1. 描述节日相关的活动或事件，考生要掌握的词组或搭配如下。

介词相关表达

a/the birthday party 生日派对	in the celebration 在庆祝中
a/the New Year's countdown 新年倒计时	on the occasion 在那时
on New Year's Day 在元旦当天	during the festival 在节日中
at the party 在派对上	on the holiday 在假期里
during the event 在活动期间	on the eve of the holiday 在假期前夕
the Spring Festival Gala 春节联欢晚会	the Dragon Boat Race 龙舟比赛

2. 时间介词in /on /at的常见用法如下。

时间介词in /on /at

in	一天中的某个阶段	**in** the morning 在早上	**in** the afternoon 在下午
	月份、季节	**in** February 在二月	**in** spring 在春天
	年份	**in** 2024 在2024年	
	其他词组	**in** three hours 三小时后	
on	一周中的某天	**on** Monday 在周一	
		on a sunny Monday 在一个晴朗的周一	
	日期	**on** 18th May 在5月18日	**on** 3rd August 在8月3日
	一些节假日	**on** New Year's Day 在元旦	
at	时刻（o'clock）	**at** 8 o'clock 在8点钟	**at** 8 a.m. 在早上8点
	weekend和night	**at** the weekend 在周末	**at** night 在晚上
	用餐时间	**at** lunchtime 在午餐时间	

百变演练

Choose the correct answer to complete the sentence. 选择正确答案填空。（代词）

1. —Can you show your new book to _____?

   —OK. Here you are.

   A. I   B. me   C. my

2. Where is your brother? I want to give _____ a book.

   A. me   B. you   C. him

3. There isn't _____ in the classroom. All the students are having a PE lesson in the

   playground.

   A. somebody   B. anybody   C. nobody

4. Believe in _____ and you can overcome your shyness.

   A. you   B. your   C. yourself

5. _____ teacher talked to _____ about the stories of the Silk Road.

   A. Our; us   B. Our; we   C. Ours; us

Day 4   聚会邀请

考场模拟

For each question, write the correct answer.

Write one word for each gap.

Example:	0	for

From:	Amy
To:	Olivia

Hi Olivia,

Thanks **(0)** _____ the invitation to your birthday party **(25)** _____ Sunday. It's
amazing to think that a year has passed since your last one.

I know your party starts **(26)** _____ 1 p.m., but I might be a bit late **(27)** _____ I have an important exam at school in the morning. I'm not sure of the way to your new house, so please text me your address. I don't want to **(28)** _____ lost on the way. I will **(29)** _____ shopping at the mall tomorrow, so it would be great if you could give me an idea of what you want for your birthday. Let **(30)** _____ know if you want me to bring anything too.

🎧 思路点拨

Step 1:【读文章，知大意】

1. 文章主旨

这是一篇Amy回复Olivia的邮件，主要介绍了Amy收到Olivia的生日邀请，并计划参加派对，同时询问了派对地址和礼物等信息。

2. 考点　考查介词、代词、连词、固定搭配和固定句型。

Step 2:【找线索，填答案】

25.【考点】介词

【解析】根据句意"谢谢你邀请我参加你星期天的生日聚会。"表示"在星期天"应该用介词on。

26.【考点】介词

【解析】此处句意为"我知道你的派对下午一点开始"。关键词1 p.m. 是"下午1点"的意思，在具体的时刻前要用介词at，比如，at ten o'clock（在10点）、at nine a.m.（在上午9点）。故正确答案为at。

27.【考点】连词

【解析】根据句意"但我可能会晚一点，_____我早上在学校有一个重要的考试。"可知空格前后为因果关系，所以要用表示原因的连接词。故正确答案为because或as。

28.【考点】固定搭配

【解析】此处句意为"我不确定去你新家的路，所以请把你的地址发短信给我。我不想在路上迷路。"表示"迷路"，可以用get lost或be lost。want to后面接动词原形。故答案为get或be。

29.【考点】固定搭配

【解析】此处句意为"我明天要去购物中心购物。" will后接动词原形，表示"去购物"，要用go shopping。故正确答案为go。

30.【考点】代词

【解析】根据句意"如果你需要我带来什么，请让我知道。"可知空格处应填写表示"我"的代词。let后面接宾语，所以用代词的宾格形式me。故正确答案为me。

【Answer key】

25. on   26. at   27. because / as   28. get / be   29. go   30. me

考点锦囊

1. 描述时间相关的表达，考生要掌握的词组或搭配如下。

时间相关表达	
at once 立即，马上	in a moment 立刻
right away 立即，马上	at the moment 此刻
without delay 毫不延迟，立即	for a moment 片刻，一会儿
without hesitation 毫不犹豫地	for a while 一会儿
in a hurry 匆忙地，立即	for the moment 暂时

2. 在邀请类信件中，还常会用到一些句型。

I'm going to... next Saturday. 我下周六要去……

Would you like to come with me? 你愿意和我一起去吗?

What about meeting at... o'clock? ……点见面怎么样?

How about meeting at the park? 公园见面怎么样?

百变演练

Choose the correct answer to complete the sentence. 选择正确答案填空。（连词）

1. You should turn off the lights _____ you leave the room.

    A. so   B. before   C. although

2. Mary cut her knee badly, _____ she didn't cry.

    A. but   B. as   C. so

3. Don't be afraid to make mistakes, _____ you'll never really learn the language.

    A. and   B. or   C. so

4. Before you get off the bus, you should wait _____ it has stopped.

    A. until   B. but   C. because

5. I want to buy something special for my grandmother, _____ her birthday is coming.

    A. because   B. although   C. so

Day 5   体育运动

 考场模拟

For each question, write the correct answer.

Write one word for each gap.

Example:	**0**	to

From:	Peter
To:	Alex

It's great that you want **(0)** _____ do a new sport. I do lots **(25)** _____ sports, but my favourite is basketball. I play twice a week at **(26)** _____ sports centre. **(27)** _____ don't you come to the sports centre with me?

From:	Alex
To:	Peter

Thank you for your invitation! I am excited to **(28)** _____ basketball with you. I am looking forward **(29)** _____ going to the sports centre and seeing if I enjoy this sport as much as you do. If there **(30)** _____ any equipment that I need to bring, please let me know.

思路点拨

Step 1:【读文章，知大意】

1. 文章主旨

这是两篇邮件。第一篇是Peter邀请Alex一起去运动中心打篮球，并鼓励他尝试新运动。第二篇是Alex接受Peter的邀请，并期待与Peter一起去运动中心打篮球，同时询问是否需要携带装备。

2. 考点　考查冠词、动词、固定搭配和固定句型。

Step 2:【找线索，填答案】

25.【考点】固定搭配

【解析】此处句意为"我做很多体育运动，但我最喜欢的是篮球。"lots of是固定搭配，意为"许多"，等于a lot of。故正确答案为of。

26.【考点】冠词

【解析】根据句意"我每周在体育中心打两次球。"可知此处指的是特定的体育中心，表示特指，用the。故正确答案为the。

27.【考点】固定句型

【解析】根据问号可知，本句为疑问句，需要用疑问词来引导。根据空格后的don't，可知空格处应填写Why，"Why don't you...?"是常用句型，意为"你为什么不……？"位于句首，首字母大写。故正确答案为Why。

28.【考点】动词

【解析】此处句意为"我很高兴和你一起打篮球。"其中play basketball是固定短语，表示"打篮球"，故正确答案是play。

29.【考点】固定搭配

【解析】look forward to是固定搭配，意为"期待"，to后面的动词用-ing形式。此处句意为"我期待着去体育中心，看看我是否像你一样喜欢这项运动。"故正确答案为to。

30.【考点】动词

【解析】此处句意为"如果我需要带什么设备，请告诉我。"分析句子结构可知，此句是there be结构。equipment意为"设备"，是不可数名词，所以be动词要用单数形式。故正确答案为is。

【Answer key】

25. of   26. the   27. Why   28. play   29. to   30. is

 考点锦囊

阅读中遇到运动相关的情景时，常会考查运动相关的动词短语。

运动	
play basketball 打篮球	go skateboarding 滑滑板
play volleyball 打排球	go swimming 去游泳
play football 踢足球	go hiking 去徒步
play baseball 打棒球	go skating 去滑冰
play badminton 打羽毛球	go skiing 去滑雪
play golf 打高尔夫球	do exercise 做运动
play tennis 打网球	take exercise 锻炼身体

百变演练

Choose the correct answer to complete the sentence. 选择正确答案填空。（动词短语）

1. In China, people usually _____ their houses to sweep away bad luck before Spring Festival.

    A. clean up   B. look up   C. make up

2. Lisa is a popular monitor. She _____ her classmates and teachers.

    A. takes part in   B. gets on well with   C. gets into trouble with

3. —Fangfang, shall we go to see a film on Saturday?

    —Sorry. I'll have to _____ my younger brother because my mother is out.

    A. look at   B. look for   C. look after

4. We have to _____ the sports meeting for the bad weather.

    A. put on   B. put up   C. put off

5. —I don't know how to _____ the old clothes.

    —You can give them away to the charity.

    A. hand in   B. deal with   C. take up

Weekend 三 每周一练

I. Circle the correct word to complete each sentence. 圈出正确的单词补全句子。

1. My birthday is **on / at** July 3rd.

2. Look! There are so many stars in **the / a** sky.

3. What **a / an** nice day! Let's go for a picnic.

4. I usually make breakfast for my family **in / on** Saturdays.

5. My best friend and **me / I** were watching TV when the rainstorm came.

6. In such cheerful conversation, the time **came / went** by all too quickly.

7. Little Mary says good night to her parents **if / before** she goes to bed every day.

8. According to the new traffic rules, people **must / may** wear a helmet when riding an e-bike.

II. Choose the correct answer to complete the sentence. 选择正确答案填空。

1. —Judy, is that boy with glasses _____ new classmate?

    —Yes. Let's say hello to _____.

    A. we; he   B. us; himself   C. our; him

2. —Mum, may I have more chocolate?

    —You'd better not _____ too much sweet food is bad for health.

    A. until   B. while   C. because

3. I have no money on me because I often pay _____ things through WeChat.

    A. to   B. of   C. for

4. There are 60 minutes in _____ hour.

    A. a   B. an   C. the

5. My mother is making _____ apple pie and I want to try _____ piece.

    A. a; an   B. a; /   C. an; a

6. I like those books! When I get my pocket money, I will buy _____.

    A. it   B. that   C. them

III. Complete the sentences with the words in the box. 用框中的单词补全句子。

| money | wash | younger | fed | our | behind |

1. It's a good habit to _____ hands before meals.

2. Alice often gives _____ to help protect wild animals.

3. Bob's grandma is eighty, but she looks much _____ than she is.

4. We believe that _____ home town will be more and more beautiful.

5. There was a playground _____ the classroom building in my school ten years ago.

6. Last summer holiday, I went fishing and _____ the pigs with my uncle.

IV. Read and choose the correct sentences to complete the conversation. 读一读，选择正确的句子补全对话。

Lucy: Hi, Tony. Do you have any plans for tomorrow?

Tony: No. Any suggestions?

Lucy: _____1_____ He is a star at the zoo and good at doing sports.

Tony: Good idea. _____2_____

Lucy: How about 8 o'clock at the zoo gate?

Tony: Sounds great. _____3_____

Lucy: I'll ride my bike. What about you?

Tony: The zoo is a little far from my home. _____4_____

Lucy: OK. _____5_____

Tony: Wonderful! We can take photos with Meng Lan together.

A. Let's bike to school.   B. Maybe I'll take a bus.

C. Then I'll take my camera.   D. How are you going there?

E. Which panda is the cutest?   F. When and where shall we meet?

G. Let's go to see the panda Meng Lan.

V. Complete the sentences according to the Chinese meanings. 根据中文提示，完成句子。

1. 多么幸运的一天!

   _____ _____ lucky day!

2. 你离开房间时必须关灯。

   You must _____ _____ the lights when you leave a room.

3. 暴风雨来临的时候，你正在做什么?

   What _____ you _____ when the rainstorm came?

4. ——谢谢你的帮助。

   ——不客气。

   —_____ you _____ your help.

   —You're welcome.

5. 你可以在字典上查阅这个单词。

   You can _____ _____ the word in the dictionary.

VI. Complete the sentences with the correct form of the words. 用所给单词的适当形式补全句子。

1. Danny is _____ (young) than his sister May.

2. It's not my book. It's _____ (her).

3. When mom came home, Peter _____ (play) the piano in the living room.

4. Last week my sister _____ (fail) her cooking exam because she burnt something.

5. We're going to make vegetable salad. How many _____ (tomato) do we need?

6. In my opinion, good friends should _____ (share) happiness or sadness with each other.

第8周目标				
学习模块	时间	主题	内容	
Mock Test	Day 1	短信息选择题	阅读模拟训练1套	☐
	Day 2	信息匹配题	阅读模拟训练1套	☐
	Day 3	阅读理解题	阅读模拟训练1套	☐
	Day 4	完形填空题	阅读模拟训练1套	☐
	Day 5	语法填空题	阅读模拟训练1套	☐

Day 1　短信息选择题

PART 1

QUESTIONS 1-6

For each question, choose the correct answer.

1
> **Closing down sale**
> **Everything must go!**
> **Save up to 40%**
> **on summer footwear.**

A You can't buy any shoes here.

B The store is closed.

C You can buy some shoes cheaper.

2
> QUIET!
> ROOM FOR STUDY ONLY
> TURN PHONES OFF
> (USE THEM IN THE
> CORRIDOR ONLY)

A Be quiet when you work in this room.

B Be quiet when you leave this room.

C Phones might not work well in the room.

3

Classes start at 8:15
each day of the week, so
remember that you need to
get to school before 8:10.
Thank you

A School start at a different time this week.

B You can get to school between 8:10 and 8:15.

C Please arrive at school early.

4

Hi Suzie,

I hope you remembered it's my party on Sunday. Let me know if you can come or not. Don't forget to bring the speakers!

Pippa

Pippa wants to know

A if Suzie went to a party last Sunday.

B if Suzie has a pair of speakers.

C if Suzie is going to the party.

5

GREEN PARK

Dogs are not allowed.
Please do not walk on the grass.
Put all litter in the bins.

A You can bring your pets here.

B You can have a picnic on the grass.

C You mustn't leave any rubbish.

6

Hi Mark,

You really helped me with Maths, I really needed it!

It's great that you've been my classroom partner this week.

Thanks a lot.

Tim

Tim is

A asking Mark for help with school work.

B thanking Mark for working with him.

C saying he wants to study with Mark.

Day 2 信息匹配题

For each question, choose the correct answer.

		Ashvani	Mirelle	Paul
7	Who does their hobby with a friend?	A	B	C
8	Who learnt their hobby from a family member?	A	B	C
9	Who has an important event next week?	A	B	C
10	Who often does their hobby alone?	A	B	C
11	Who is excited about doing their hobby during the holidays?	A	B	C
12	Who sometimes feels anxious when they do their hobby?	A	B	C
13	Who attends a club once a week?	A	B	C

My favourite hobby

Ashvani

I play football with the Under 13s club in my city. We play on Mondays and Fridays and we usually have matches every Saturday. I'm the goalkeeper and I sometimes worry when we have a match. But our coach is very friendly and he has helped me a lot. We've got a big match next week. If we win it, we win the whole competition. Our coach says we can have a big party after the match – it's doesn't matter if we win or lose.

Mirelle

I do gymnastics twice during the week and on Saturday mornings. All together it's 11 hours a week! It's quite a lot, I know. But I love it! My best friend Emma also does it. She's a year older than me and she's amazing at it. This summer Emma and I are going to summer camp together. There will be some gymnastics, but other activities too. I'm so excited!

Paul

I play chess in my spare time and I'm quite good. I first learned it from my cousin Neal. But he doesn't live in my town so we can't play together very often. No one else in my family plays so I play on my computer. I'm also in the chess club at school – it's every Tuesday afternoon. I'm going to participate in a chess competition next month. I hope I win!

Day 3   阅读理解题

PART 3

QUESTIONS 14-18

For each question, choose the correct answer.

The best ice cream in town

The Golden Pineapple is a place that sells ice cream. It opened last week in the centre of Fleet, a seaside town between Shoreham and Hastings. I was one of the first customers. The name comes from the lights hanging from the ceiling. They look like golden pineapples.

The owners, John and Jane, were very friendly and invited me to try all the different flavours. There was chocolate, lemon, lime and, of course, pineapple. It is their bestselling ice cream. Jane and John told me how they started to make ice cream. They lived in Oliva, a town in Spain, for three years and loved eating ice cream in the hot weather. They decided to find out how to make it. They worked in an ice cream shop there. After ten weeks of hard work, they knew exactly what to do.

They came back to the UK six months ago and found a shop in a street where many people walk past every day. They put in the machines they needed to make the ice cream and decorated the shop. They were finally ready to open. The ice creams they sell are quite cheap. I think it is a great place to go to with a group of friends and try as many types of ice cream as you can. The ice cream shop is open every day from 9 a.m. to 6 p.m. except Wednesday when it is closed all day. In July and August, it stays open until 8 p.m.

Next year, Jane and John are planning to open another ice cream shop. It will be in the same town but much closer to the beach. They hope to be very busy, even though the weather will not be as good as it is in Spain!

14 The shop sells

   A pineapple ice cream.

   B various types of fruit.

   C various flavours of ice cream.

15 The owners

   A are Spanish.

   B have lived in Spain for ten weeks.

   C spent three years in Spain.

16 The ice cream shop is in a

   A busy street.

   B supermarket.

   C car park.

17 You cannot buy ice cream on

   A Mondays.

   B Wednesdays.

   C Fridays.

18 Why does the speaker like the Golden Pineapple?

   A Because ice cream is cheap.

   B Because it is open until 8 p.m.

   C Because you can go with friends and try a lot of flavours.

完形填空题

PART 4

QUESTIONS 19-24

For each question, choose the correct answer.

SUMMER COURSES FOR STUDENTS!

Come and **(19)** .... part in our exciting summer courses! We are offering many different activities which we know you will enjoy. There are **(20)** .... where you can draw and paint and learn about famous artists.

You can **(21)** .... your sports skills in our tennis, football and athletics classes. Would you **(22)** .... to spend time in the swimming pool learning **(23)** .... to dive and swim under water? Try our swimming courses. We accept students from 12 to 17 for all our courses and we can offer a special **(24)** .... for July and August this year.

To find out more, visit our website: www.summercourses.org.

---

19 A bring   B take   C give

20 A classes   B rooms   C schools

21 A increase   B learn   C improve

22 A want   B like   C know

23 A what   B when   C how

24 A cost   B price   C offer

Day 5 语法填空题

PART 5

QUESTIONS 25-30

For each question, write the correct answer.

Write **ONE** word for each gap.

Example:

0	on

From:	Olivia
To:	Nat

Hi Nat!

I'm **(0)** .... holiday with my family **(25)** .... India. The weather is sunny and hot today, but yesterday it rained all day. We're staying **(26)** .... a hotel which is next **(27)** .... the beach, and we go swimming in the sea and the swimming pool every day.

The food here is very good. We went **(28)** .... for dinner yesterday evening and had some delicious seafood.

There is a park near the hotel where **(29)** .... can sit under the lemon trees.

I've got a necklace for you which I bought from the market! I'll give it to you next week. I hope **(30)** .... like it.

See you soon,

Olivia

附录　参考答案

Week 2

Day 2
1. apple   2. doctor   3. bus
4. sister   5. cake   6. flower

Day 3
1. C   2. C   3. C   4. C   5. B   6. B

Day 4
1. C   2. A   3. A   4. B   5. C   6. B   7. B   8. B

Day 5
1. A   2. C   3. A   4. B   5. C   6. A

Weekend
I.   1. too   2. hungry   3. curious
    4. busy   5. badly   6. outgoing
II.   1. C   2. B   3. C   4. C   5. C   6. A   7. C   8. C
III.   1. an   2. 不填; the   3. a
    4. a   5. the   6. the; a
IV.   1. to   2. in   3. between
    4. from   5. behind   6. in
    7. on   8. in
V.   1. waste   2. put away   3. look after
    4. pick   5. find out

Week 3

Day 1
1. A   2. A   3. C   4. B   5. C

Day 2
1. A   2. B   3. C   4. B   5. A

Day 3
1. A   2. B   3. A   4. C   5. C

Day 4
1. B   2. C   3. C   4. A   5. B

Day 5
1. C   2. C   3. B   4. A   5. B

Weekend
I.   1. she   2. at   3. so   4. clearly
    5. trust   6. forty   7. for   8. or
II.   1. C   2. C   3. C   4. B   5. A   6. B
III.   1. seasons   2. yourself   3. bottles
    4. instead of   5. silent   6. repeats
IV.   1. E   2. F   3. B   4. A   5. C   6. D
V.   1. your   2. strawberries
    3. to answer   4. sat
    5. Chinese   6. was invented
VI.   1. to play   2. in surprise   3. so; that
    4. why; late   5. don't; likes

Week 4

Day 2
I.   1. notebooks   2. was   3. friendly
    4. reading   5. twice
II.   1. Last/family name
    2. made friends   3. so; that
    4. Have; read   5. telling stories
III.   1. T   2. F   3. T   4. F   5. F

Day 4
I.   1. Make   2. to circle   3. trying
    4. fresher   5. buildings
II.   1. take part in   2. if she could do
    3. the oldest   4. either; or
    5. had difficulty in making
III.   1. T   2. F   3. T   4. F   5. T

Day 6
I.   1. comes   2. carelessly   3. hearing
    4. rainy   5. danger
II.   1. How happy   2. to know

3. by mistake　　4. used to

5. take; miss

III. 1. F　　2. F　　3. T　　4. T　　5. T

Weekend

I. 1. greeted　　2. protect　　3. clean

4. lucky　　5. during

II. 1. between; and　　2. Follow/obey; traffic

3. prefer singers　　4. fall off

5. spend; with

III. 1. C　2. A　3. B　4. C　5. A　6. B　7. C

Week 5

Day 2

I. 1. was invited　　2. dancing; practice

3. exciting　　4. making

5. married

II. 1. about　2. for　3. in　4. of　5. for

III. 1. T　　2. F　　3. F　　4. F　　5. T

Day 4

I. 1. were greeted　　2. taste

3. highly　　4. saw

5. photos

II. 1. of　2. from　3. into　4. with　5. with

III. 1. T　　2. F　　3. T　　4. T　　5. F

Day 6

I. 1. playing　　2. throw　　3. sharing

4. youngest　　5. are invited

II. 1. 她有一个巨大的花园，每年可以产出超过100磅的食物！

2. 肯德尔尝试了一下，惊讶地发现小土豆长出了新的叶子。

3. 不久之后，她的父母在后院建了一个小花园。

4. 肯德尔成为其他孩子的楷模。

5. 种植食物需要很多工作，但只要大家共同努力，就能做到。

III. 1. F　　2. T　　3. F　　4. T　　5. F

Weekend

I. 1. How often　2. Where　　3. When

4. What　　5. Why

II. 1. Why did he join the dance club?

2. How did she feel about moving to a new school?

3. He is sorry he didn't try harder.

4. There should be more signs along the trail.

5. I have already finished my breakfast.

III. 1. B　　2. C　　3. A　　4. C　　5. C

Week 6

Day 1

1. C　　2. C　　3. B　　4. C　　5. B

Day 2

1. A　　2. A　　3. A　　4. C　　5. B

Day 3

1. A　　2. C　　3. A　　4. B　　5. C

Day 4

1. C　　2. C　　3. A　　4. A　　5. B

Day 5

1. C　　2. A　　3. B　　4. B　　5. C

Weekend

I. 1. clear　　2. lonely　　3. awful

4. tired　　5. never　　6. faster

7. carefully　　8. polite

II. 1. C　2. C　3. C　4. A　5. A　6. C

III. 1. point　　2. borrowed　3. sounds

4. drawing　　5. turn　　6. get

IV. 1. E　　2. D　　3. G　　4. B　　5. A

V. 1. make friends

2. important; practise/practice

3. come true

4. more; more

5. work hard

VI. 1. third　　　　2. patiently

3. to shake   4. have learned
5. stamps   6. tell

Week 7

Day 1
1. A   2. C   3. A   4. B   5. C

Day 2
1. B   2. C   3. C   4. B   5. C

Day 3
1. B   2. C   3. B   4. C   5. A

Day 4
1. B   2. A   3. B   4. A   5. A

Day 5
1. A   2. B   3. C   4. C   5. B

Weekend
I.   1. on   2. the   3. a   4. on
     5. I   6. went   7. before   8. must
II. 1. C   2. C   3. C   4. B   5. C   6. C
III. 1. wash   2. money   3. younger
     4. our   5. behind   6. fed
IV. 1. G   2. F   3. D   4. B   5. C
V.   1. What a   2. turn off
     3. were; doing   4. Thank; for
     5. look up
VI. 1. younger   2. hers
     3. was playing   4. failed
     5. tomatoes   6. share

Week 8

Day 1
[Key] 1. C   2. A   3. C   4. C   5. C   6. B
[答案详解]

1. 该题文本是一则通知，通知内容为一家商店"清仓大甩卖"。根据通知中的footwear（鞋类）可知，该店在促销鞋类商品，故A选项说的"你在这里买不到鞋"错误，排除A。通知的标题为Closing down sale，意为"清仓大甩卖"，并未说"商店关门了"，故B错误。通知中提到Save up to 40% on summer footwear.（夏季鞋款最高可节省40%。）即"鞋子正在搞促销活动"，所以C描述的"你可以买到一些便宜的鞋"与通知内容一致，故选C。

2. 该题文本是一条标识语，用于说明该房间的使用规则，即"需要保持安静！该房间仅供学习使用。手机需要保持关闭（仅在走廊里可以使用手机）。"A选项提到"在这个房间里干活的时候要保持安静"，符合标识语的内容；B选项"在你离开这个房间的时候要保持安静"，在标识语中未提到，故排除；C选项"手机在房间里可能信号不好"，标识语中只是要求在房间里不能使用手机，故排除；正确答案为A。

3. 该题文本是一则通知，告诉学生开始上课的时间以及到校的时间。每天上课时间为8:15，学生需要在8:10前到校。A选项"本周上课时间不同"，通知中已经说明了Classes start at 8:15 each day of the week.（这周的每天都是8:15上课。）故A可排除；B选项"你可以在8:10到8:15之间到校"，通知中已经说明要在8:10之前到校，故排除B；C选项"请早些时间到校"，符合通知的内容，故选C。

4. 该题文本是一则Pippa写给的Suzie的消息留言。留言内容大意为"Pippa的派对在周日，Pippa想知道Suzie是否能来，同时提醒Suzie别忘了带speakers（扬声器）"。A选项中说的是last Sunday（上周日），不符合信息内容，故可排除；B选项说"Suzie是否有一副扬声器"，而留言消息中只是提醒

Suzie要记得带，没有问她有没有，故可排除；C选项说"Suzie是否可以来派对"符合消息内容，故选C。

5. 该题文本是一条标识语，说明Green Park的一些要求：狗不准入内；不要在草地上走；将所有垃圾扔进垃圾桶。A选项提到"你可以带宠物来这里"，但是标识语的第一条就是"狗不准入内"，故可排除；B选项提到"你可以在草地上野餐"，标识语的第二条就是"不允许在草坪上行走"，故可排除；C选项"你不能留下任何垃圾"，选项中的rubbish和标识语中的litter同义，两句意思相近，故C为正确答案。

6. 该题文本是Tim写给Mark的一则表达感谢的消息留言。留言第一句说"你真的帮助了我的数学，我真的很需要。"注意这里用的是过去式helped和needed，所以是已经发生了的事情，故A选项"Tim正在向Mark寻求作业上的帮助"不正确，可排除；留言中第二句说"这周你一直是我的课堂搭档，真是太好了。"该句中使用了现在完成时have been，讲述的也是过去发生的事情，所以C选项"Tim说他想和Mark一起学习"也不符合，故可排除；留言前两句结合结尾的Thanks a lot.（十分感谢。）可知Tim是在感谢Mark和他一起学习，故B选项为正确答案。

Day 2

[Key] 7. B 8. C 9. A 10. C
11. B 12. A 13. C

[答案详解]

7. 题目询问"谁和朋友一起做自己爱做的事情？"Ashvani在介绍自己的兴趣爱好时，提到是参加的一个club；……介绍时，提到了自己最好的朋

友Emma，她们两个人都喜欢体操，并且会一起参加一个夏令营，夏令营里也有体操活动；Paul介绍时，提到首先他是从他的堂兄弟那里学会的下象棋，后来是在电脑上玩，他还参加了学校的象棋俱乐部。由此得知，和朋友一起做自己爱做的事情的是Mirelle，故本题选B。

8. 题目询问"谁从家庭成员那里学会了他们的爱好？"根据文章信息，Paul在介绍自己的兴趣爱好"下象棋"时提到I first learned it from my cousin Neal.（我第一次是从我的堂兄弟Neal那里学会的。）cousin就属于题干中提到的family member，故本题选C。

9. 题目询问"谁下周有重要活动？"注意题干中的关键词next week，三个人物介绍中只有Ashvani提到We've got a big match next week.（我们下周有场重要比赛。）句中的a big match和题干中的an important event同义，由此得知，本题应选A。

10. 题目询问"谁经常独自去做自己的爱好？"文章中Paul在描述时，提到自己首次学习象棋，是跟自己的堂兄弟Neal学的，但是后面又提到But he doesn't live in my town so we can't play together very often. No one else in my family plays so I play on my computer.（但他不住在我的城里，所以我们不能经常一起玩。我家里没有其他人玩，所以我在电脑上玩。）由此推断出，Paul在玩象棋的时候，经常是自己去跟电脑玩，故选C。

11. 题目询问"谁对在假期里去做自己的爱好感到兴奋？"根据题干中的关键词excited可以定位到原文中Mirelle的描述：This summer Emma and I are going to summer camp... I'm so excited.

其中提到的summer指代的就是题干中的holiday，由此可知，正确答案是B。

12. 题目询问"当他们做自己的爱好时，谁有时会感到焦虑？"Ashvani在介绍时提到，I'm the goalkeeper and I sometimes worry when we have a match.（我是守门员，比赛时我有时会担心。）句中的worry和题干中的anxious意思相近，故选A。

13. 题目询问"谁每周参加一次俱乐部？"文章中Ashvani参加的俱乐部是Mondays and Fridays（周一和周五），并且每周六有比赛，故不是Ashvani；Mirelle在开头就提到I do gymnastics twice during the week and on Saturday mornings.（周中是两次，还有星期六的上午。）所以Mirelle也不是每周参加一次俱乐部；Paul在介绍象棋俱乐部时提到，I'm also in the chess club at school – it's every Tuesday afternoon.（我也参加学校的象棋俱乐部，时间是每周二的下午。）所以Paul是每周参加一次俱乐部，故选C。

Day 3

[Key] 14. C 15. C 16. A 17. B 18. C
[答案详解]

14. 文章开头就介绍了The Golden Pineapple is a place that sells ice cream.（名为"金菠萝"的商店是一个卖冰激凌的地方。）故B选项可排除。在第二段中又提到all the different flavours（所有不同的味道），并且后面提到了巧克力、柠檬、橙子还有菠萝等味道，所以该店售卖的应该是"各种口味的冰激凌"。

15. 文章第二段中提到They lived in Oliva, a town in Spain, for three years.（他们

在西班牙的奥利瓦镇住了三年。）句中的they指代的就是第二段开头提到的the owners, John and Jane。由此得知，店主在西班牙住了三年，也就是C选项中提到的"在西班牙待了三年"，故选C。

16. 文章第三段中提到They came back to the UK six months ago and found a shop in a street where many people walk past every day.（六个月前，他们回到英国，在一条街上发现了一家商店，每天都有很多人经过。）在描述street时，用了一个where引导的定语从句，即where many people walk past every day，其含义相当于A选项的busy street（繁忙的街道），故本题选A。

17. 文章中第三段最后在描述店铺营业时间时，提到The ice cream shop is open every day from 9 a.m. to 6 p.m. except Wednesday when it is closed all day.（这家冰激凌店每天早上9点到下午6点营业，星期三全天不营业。）由此得知，在星期三买不到冰激凌，故选B。

18. 文章中第三段作者在表述自己的想法时提到I think it is a great place to go to with a group of friends and try as many types of ice cream as you can.（我认为这是一个很好的地方，可以和一群朋友一起去，可以尝试各种口味的冰激凌。）句中的many types of ice cream指的就是C选项中的a lot of flavours（很多口味），故选C。

Day 4

[Key] 19. B 20. A 21. C 22. B 23. C 24. B
[答案详解]

19. 考查固定搭配。根据下一句提到的"我们提供许多不同的活动，我们知道你会喜欢的。"再结合标题，可知

151

该文章是关于"课程招生"的,空格后是part in,三个选项中,只有take可以与其构成固定搭配take part in,表示"参加"的意思,补充后,整句话的意思是"来参加我们激动人心的夏季课程吧!"故本题选B。

20. 考查名词辨析。空格后面是where引导的定语从句,空格处需填入where所代表的先行词,根据定语从句中的描述,在"这里",you can draw and paint and learn about famous artists(你可以画画,了解著名艺术家),结合文意,此处应指的是"课程",A选项可表示"课程",B选项指"房间",C选项指"学校",故正确答案为A。

21. 考查动词辨析。空格所在处的句意为"你可以在我们的网球、足球和田径课上_____你的运动技能。"三个选项中,increase表示"增加",offer表示"提供",improve表示"提高",和skill常一起使用的动词是improve,故选C。

22. 考查动词辨析。空格所在处是一个问句,根据下一句Try our swimming courses.(试试我们的游泳课程。)可知,本句是在询问读者是否愿意参加游泳课程,询问意愿时常会用句型Would you like to...?故本题选B。

23. 考查关系副词。空格所在处的句意为"你愿意花时间在泳池学习_____潜水和在水下游泳吗?"三个选项,what表示"什么",when表示"什么时候",how表示"如何",其中how最符合句意,故本题选C。

查名词辨析。空格所在处的句意为_____年7月和8月我们可以提供特殊的

_____。"三个选项都是和"钱"相关,结合句意,此处要表达的是"特价",special price表示"优惠价格"的意思,故选B。

Day 5

[Key] 25. in   26. in   27. to
      28. out   29. we   30. you

[答案详解]

25. 考查介词。空格后面是地名India,结合句意"我和家人一起在印度度假"可知,表示"在印度"使用介词in。

26. 考查介词。空格所在处句意为"我们住在宾馆",表示"住宾馆"时,stay后面要用介词in,即stay in a hotel,故填in。

27. 考查介词。该空格所在处为which引导的定语从句中,该定语从句修饰hotel,说明的是hotel的位置,be next to为"紧邻着",故填入to。

28. 考查介词。空格所在处句意为"我们昨天_____吃饭,吃了一些美味的海鲜。"结合句意,此处应表示"外出用餐",go out for dinner为固定搭配,故此处应填入out。

29. 考查代词。空格处于where引导的定语从句中,空格后面can sit是谓语,本句缺少主语。再结合前文中在描述度假的情况时,用的主语都是we,故此处也应填入we,补充后,该句句意为"宾馆附近有一个公园,我们可以坐在柠檬树下。"

30. 考查代词。根据前两句的句意"我从市场上买了一条项链给你!我下星期给你。"可知,I(写信的人)给you(读信的人)买了一条项链,所以是希望"读信的人"喜欢,故空格处应填入you。